Nobel's Women of Peace

The Women's Hall of Fame Series

Nobel's Women of
PEACE

Michelle Benjamin
& Maggie Mooney

Second Story Press

Library and Archives Canada Cataloguing in Publication

Benjamin, Michelle
Nobel's women of peace / by Michelle Benjamin and Maggie Mooney.

(The women's hall of fame series)

ISBN 978-1-897187-38-8

1. Women Nobel Prize winners—Biography. 2. Women pacifists—
Biography. I. Mooney, Maggie, 1957- II. Title. III. Series: Women's hall of
fame series

JZ5540.B45 2008   303.6'60922   C2008-905903-4

Edited by Colin Thomas
Designed by Melissa Kaita
Cover illustration and icons © istockphoto.com
Printed and bound in Canada

Mixed Sources
Product group from well-managed
forests and other controlled sources
www.fsc.org Cert no. SW-COC-001326
© 1996 Forest Stewardship Council

*Second Story Press gratefully acknowledges the support of the Ontario Arts Council
and the Canada Council for the Arts for our publishing program. We acknowledge
the financial support of the Government of Canada through the Book Publishing
Industry Development Program.*

 ONTARIO ARTS COUNCIL
CONSEIL DES ARTS DE L'ONTARIO   Canada Council   Conseil des Arts
for the Arts   du Canada

Published by
Second Story Press
20 Maud Street, Suite 401
Toronto, ON
M5V 2M5
www.secondstorypress.ca

CONTENTS

INTRODUCTION   1

Bertha von Suttner   5

Jane Addams   15

Emily Greene Balch   27

Betty Williams & Máiread Corrigan Maguire   37

Mother Teresa   49

Alva Myrdal   63

Aung San Suu Kyi   73

Rigoberta Menchú Tum   87

Jody Williams   99

Shirin Ebadi   109

Wangari Maathai   121

WHAT YOU CAN DO   131

SOURCES AND RESOURCES   135

PHOTO CREDITS   145

ACKNOWLEDGMENTS   146

For our friends in Máncora, Peru—especially Elena and Benjamin—who inspired us while we wrote this book, and who fill their world (and ours) with love and courage. Mucho amor, estimados amigos.

And for Caitlin, our hero.

Introduction

"The person who shall have done the most or the best work for fraternity between nations."

Alva Myrdal, who won the Nobel Peace Prize in 1982, said of its founder, "[Alfred] Nobel was a genuine friend of peace. He even went so far as to believe that he had invented a tool of destruction, dynamite, which would make war so senseless that it would become impossible. He was wrong."

The Nobel Peace Prize is the world's most prestigious honor. It is given to courageous and dedicated people who have committed their lives to working for peace, for human rights, and democracy: people who have tried to make the world a safer and more healthy place.

But Alfred Nobel (1833-1896), who established the award, was the inventor of dynamite and nitroglycerin. He was also many other things. He was a shrewd Swedish businessman and scientist who was fluent in several languages, wrote romantic poetry and plays, and—despite his technological contributions to warfare—was deeply interested in peace and disarmament. His friend Bertha von Suttner, the first woman to win the Peace Prize, described Alfred like this: "A thinker, a poet, a man both kindly and bitter, unhappy and light-hearted, given to superb flights of mind and to malicious suspicions, passionately in love with the far horizons of human thoughts and profoundly distrustful of the pettiness of human folly, understanding everything and hoping for nothing."

Clearly, Alfred was concerned about how he would be remembered after his death. An obituary appeared in error almost ten years before his actual death (it was his brother Ludwig who had died). This mistake may have inspired some of Alfred's desire to leave a positive legacy. The obituary claimed, *"Le marchand de la mort est mort"*—the merchant of death is dead—and went on to say, "Dr. Alfred Nobel, who became rich by finding ways to kill more people faster than ever before, died yesterday."

Alfred truly, and somewhat naively, saw his inventions as a way to stop war. He said to Bertha, "My factories may make an end to war sooner than your [peace] congresses . . . The day when two Army corps can annihilate each other in one second, all civilized nations, it is hoped, will recoil from war and discharge their troops."

Before his death, Alfred realized how misguided these optimistic sentiments were, and he concluded that knowledge was the single most important necessity in the quest for peace. When Alfred did die, on December 10, 1896, he left most of his substantial fortune to a new foundation that was instructed to award people who have done their best for humanity in the fields of physics, chemistry, physiology or medicine, literature, and peace.

Rather than being known as the merchant of death, Nobel is remembered for the support he has given to important pursuits. The Peace Prize, according to Alfred's instructions, is given to "the person who shall have done the most or the best work for fraternity between nations, for the abolition or reduction of standing armies and for the holding and promotion of peace congresses." These criteria have been expanded over the years to include disarmament, humanitarian work, and environmental activism, and the Nobel Peace Prize is awarded to organizations as well as to individuals.

Alfred Nobel

The first Nobel Peace Prize was bestowed on December 10, 1901. Since then—and always on December 10, the date of Alfred's death—ninety-five individuals and twenty organizations have received the Prize. Only twelve women have been selected to receive the honor (two women, Betty Williams and Máiread Corrigan Maguire, received it together in the same year).

The low representation of women among Nobel Peace Prize laureates is curious, especially in light of how active women have been in the international peace movement over the last hundred years. Many anti-war organizations and humanitarian causes, including the Women's International League for Peace and Freedom, the International Campaign to Ban Landmines and the Green Belt Movement, have been inspired, started, and run by women. The trend, however, has changed. While only four women were honored in the first seventy years that the prize was awarded, it has been given to women seven times in the last thirty years.

The twelve inspiring women who have received the Nobel Peace Prize have been similar in spirit and motivation, but very different in their lives and experiences. They come from a range of countries, from different classes—some were rich and others were very poor—and diverse family backgrounds, as well as different religious and spiritual beliefs.

The common thread that connects these women, however, is their remarkable courage, their dedication to making the world a better place, and their willingness to work hard. They have often made great sacrifices in their efforts against war and on behalf of human rights, and they have never given up, even in the face of tremendous hardship. They have all been strong feminists who have spoken out on behalf of women's rights, and who have recognized that peace, human rights, and democracy are inextricably linked. They inspire us to be the very best, and to do what we can to make the world a better, safer place.

Jody Williams, who was awarded the Nobel Peace Prize in 1997 for her work to rid the world of landmines, said, "Please, use your individual power . . . for change. Seize that power and go forth as troublemakers for positive change on our very small planet." Sometimes it takes a troublemaker, someone who isn't afraid to stand up and fight for what they believe in, to make positive things happen in the world. These twelve incredible women were definitely troublemakers who worked for peace, justice, and equality. Without a doubt, each one of them would encourage you to go out and do the same.

Bertha von Suttner

Nobel Peace
Prize Laureate, 1905

"Peace Bertha": The Generalissimo of the Peace Movement

Bertha von Suttner was beautiful, accomplished, and, in her early years, in great need of money. It would have been easy for her to marry for money and disappear into obscurity. But Bertha was too principled—and too passionate—to let that happen. She married for love and, appalled by the cruelties of war, she became a pioneering pacifist and one of the most famous and influential women of her time.

Countess Bertha Felicie Sofie Kinsky von Chinic und Tettau, or Bertha Kinsky, was born on June 9, 1843 in Prague, which is now in the Czech Republic, but then was

Across Europe, buildings, streets, awards, and associations are named after Bertha von Suttner. She was honored by her birth country in 2002, when her image was used on the Austrian two-Euro coin.

part of the Austrian Empire. Her father was a field marshal who died before she was born. He left her mother with a small income, so she was able to provide Bertha with a governess and a solid education. Bertha spoke four languages—English, French, German, and Italian—and studied the works of the great philosophers and sci-entists. She also loved music, and hoped to become a famous singer until she realized that performing in front of an audience terrified her.

Bertha and her mother traveled frequently, often to the fashionable casinos and spas of Paris, Rome, and Venice, where Bertha's mother frivolously spent their limited funds at gambling tables and parties. Because she was a child, Bertha was not permitted into the casinos and clubs, so she spent many evenings alone in hotel rooms. She didn't mind. She always had a collection of books with her, and enjoyed having time alone to read and write.

Bertha was classically beautiful and charming, with brightly expressive eyes and thick, dark hair. By age thirteen, she was already turning down marriage proposals. She avoided marrying two rich, older men who were drawn to her beauty and intelligence, but for whom she had no affection. When she was twenty-nine, however, she accepted the proposal of Prince Adolf Wittgenstein. They both enjoyed singing, and imagined a life together as musicians. Tragically, Prince Adolf died at sea before they were wed.

At a young age Bertha had understood that she would have to learn to support herself, and by the time she was thirty, when she and her mother were living in Vienna, she realized that her family's financial situation had become precarious. Bertha took a job as a teacher and governess to four young girls in the von Suttner family. The girls were enchanted with their talented and beautiful new governess, as was their older brother Arthur. Soon, Bertha and twenty-three-year-old Arthur von Suttner were in love and planning to marry.

Arthur's parents did not approve. Not only was Bertha seven years older than Arthur, but her mother was a gambler! Arthur's parents had hoped that his bride would come with a valuable dowry to help increase the family's dwindling fortunes. They would not permit the relationship with Bertha to continue.

After a tearful farewell, Bertha left Vienna for Paris. Full of grief, but knowing that she needed to forget Arthur and become financially independent, Bertha responded to an advertisement in the newspaper: "A very wealthy, highly educated, older gentleman living in Paris seeks a lady well-versed in languages, also elderly, as secretary and manager of his household."

The "older gentleman" was forty-two-year-old businessman and scientist Alfred Nobel, the inventor of dynamite. Impressed by Bertha's skill with languages, he was soon captivated by her nimble mind. Affection developed between them very quickly, and within one week Alfred asked if "her heart was taken." Bertha confessed her love for Arthur, and admitted her reasons for leaving Vienna.

Alfred and Bertha engaged in many lively conversations. She learned of his literary and scientific interests, and came to understand his enormous wealth and the responsibilities that came with it. This was a time of relative peace in Europe, and Bertha had not yet developed her passionate interest in the peace movement. But she enjoyed hearing Alfred's hopes that his inventions would be "so frightfully effective and devastating that it would forever make wars altogether impossible." The idea of putting an end to war became central to their friendship, which would last the rest of their lives.

Only a few days after she had left Vienna, Bertha received a pleading telegram from Arthur. In it he cried, "I cannot live without thee!" When Alfred left Paris on a business trip, Bertha decided she must follow her heart. Giving up the secure income that a life with Alfred Nobel would have provided, she sold a valuable diamond pin that she had recently inherited, bought a train ticket back to Vienna, and returned to Arthur. Shortly after, in June 1876, the couple married in secret.

Bertha and Arthur fled Vienna and his family's disapproval, and lived for the next nine years in Russia. There, they met up with Ekaterina Dadiani, Princess of Mingrelia, an older friend and mentor from Bertha's childhood. Through their connections with the princess, they each obtained employment—Bertha taught languages and music, while Arthur worked as a secretary and architect. In the evenings, invited by the princess, they attended social events with local nobility.

Despite the princess' support, the couple struggled financially. Bertha said in her memoirs, "We got to know the ghost of 'Hunger'." But they were in love and happy to be together, and faced their hardships with humor and strength.

In 1877, Russia declared war on Turkey, and Bertha and Arthur volunteered at a nearby hospital. Both were horrified and deeply affected by the injured and dying soldiers. They attempted to enlist in the medical service but learned

that they would have to work in different locations. Disappointed, but unwilling to be separated, Bertha and Arthur withdrew their services.

Now even deeper in poverty, they decided to try their hand at professional writing. Arthur wrote articles about the miseries of the war that were published across Europe. Bertha's work also started to appear in newspapers and journals. Her first full-length book, *Inventory of a Soul,* was an exploration of the ideas of the major thinkers of the day, including those of Charles Darwin.

In 1885, Bertha and Arthur returned to Vienna and reconciled with Arthur's family. By this time, they were making a regular income from their literary work, and found themselves having to support Arthur's family, which had lost its fortune. Bertha and Arthur were also paying off debts left by Bertha's mother, who had died in 1884.

"You, Madame Baroness, have taken the lead among women of today. You have attacked war itself and cried to the nations: 'Down with arms!' This call will be your eternal honor."
—Jørgen Gunnarsson Løvland, Chairman of the Nobel Committee, in his presentation speech to Bertha von Sutter on April 18, 1906.

During Bertha's nine years in Russia, she and Alfred Nobel had carried on a lively correspondence in French, English, and German. In 1887, Alfred invited Bertha and Arthur to visit him in Paris and introduced them to a group of the most original writers and thinkers in the city. Their conversations often circled around the political tensions between France and Germany, as well as issues of peace and disarmament.

Through her new friends, Bertha learned of the International Arbitration and Peace Association (IAPA), a recently founded London-based organization. She became preoccupied with this group, in particular its goal of forming an international league that would arbitrate disputes and work towards peace between countries, much like the United Nations does today. As she later recalled, "This information electrified me."

Bertha discussed her growing interest in the peace movement in *The Machine Age*, which was published in 1889. It also dealt with the issues of women's rights, education, and nationalism. Aware that this highly intellectual work might be received less seriously if written by a woman, she published it under the pseudonym "Jemand," which in German means "someone." The book was an enormous success.

The income from *The Machine Age* provided Bertha and Arthur with enough money to move to Paris. Here she wrote and published *Lay Down Your Arms: The Autobiography of Maria von Tilling*. This fictional story of a woman who suffered tragic losses through four wars was embraced by readers across Europe and around the world, propelling Bertha to the front lines of the anti-war movement.

The novel's influence was remarkable: it was produced in thirty-five editions in Germany alone, translated into almost every European language, and in 1914 it was made into a film. Bertha's publisher, who had been skeptical about the book and had to be convinced to publish it, could barely keep up with the demand. The book and the response to it invigorated the international peace movement. Alfred Nobel wrote to congratulate Bertha, and said that he wanted to shake her hand, "that hand of an Amazon who so valiantly makes war on war."

Bertha was praised for her revolutionary thinking and courage. As countries were building up arms in anticipation of war, Bertha not only criticized the military, but—through her fictional characters—also expressed optimism for peace. And perhaps most courageously, she offered a woman's perspective on the horrors of war. The enormous success of *Lay Down Your Arms* made it clear to Bertha that the general public was eager to hear messages of peace. Bertha was convinced that this—using her talents and energy in support of the peace movement—was her life's work.

Alfred Nobel

From then on, most of Bertha's energy and writing were enthusiastically devoted to the crusade for disarmament. She wrote reports and pamphlets, and lectured to promote peace projects. She launched the Austrian Peace Society and established the fund for the Bern Peace Bureau in Bern, Switzerland—a central office through which the pacifist activities of several countries were coordinated. She also spoke passionately for the development of an organization like the United Nations and envisioned peacekeeping forces like the ones that exist today.

But perhaps the most important legacy that she left involved the influence that she exerted on her friend Alfred Nobel. She worked hard to persuade him to share his substantial riches with the peace movement. Nobel was often skeptical about anti-war ideas such as disarmament, and had his own thoughts on the best way to secure peace. But he remained interested in Bertha's work. In one letter, he promised, "If you keep me in touch with developments, and if I hear that the Peace Movement is moving along the road of

The Bertha von Suttner monument in Wagga Wagga, Australia

practical activity, then I will help it on with money."

Bertha kept after him. "Don't always call our peace plan a dream," she wrote to him. "Progress towards justice is surely not a dream. It is the law of civilization." Nobel responded with generous donations.

In 1893, during Arthur and Bertha's final visit with Alfred, the three of them discussed how Alfred could guarantee that his money would continue to do good after his death. Alfred took this

At the 1899 Hague Peace Conference, Bertha suggested that the terms "pacifism" and "pacifist" be adopted to replace the numerous other names such as "friends of peace" and "followers of peace." The words are still in common usage today.

conversation to heart. He died in 1896, and in his final will, inspired by the life and work of Bertha von Suttner, he left instructions for a prize that would be given "to the person who shall have done the most or the best work for the fraternity between nations, for the abolition or reduction of standing armies, and for the holding of peace congresses." Thanks largely to the influence of Bertha von Suttner, the Nobel Peace Prize, the most important award in the world, was established.

Despite personal financial hardships, Bertha and Arthur continued to work together to free the world of war. They lectured, wrote, organized, and lobbied on local and international levels, with both grassroots organizations and government. Arthur died in 1902 and, though grief-stricken, Bertha was determined to carry on their work. She traveled extensively, including a lecture tour of the United States, where she met American President Theodore Roosevelt and spoke at the Boston Peace Congress.

In 1903, a Berlin newspaper poll determined that

Bertha—now often known as "Peace Bertha"—was one of the five "most famous women," an honor she shared with entertainers and royalty. And two years later, Bertha von Suttner was awarded the Nobel Peace Prize. The first medal had been awarded in 1901; Bertha was the first woman and fifth person to receive the honor. Many thought that she should have received the first prize, or the second, but she was gracious when the award was announced, and grateful for the money. Her only sadness was that she was not able to share the recognition with her beloved Arthur.

In her Nobel lecture, Bertha said, "Up to the present time, the military organization of our society has been founded upon a denial of the possibility of peace, a contempt for the value of human life, and an acceptance of the urge to kill." And then she expressed hope: "It is erroneous to believe that the future will of necessity continue the trends of the past and the present."

The honor and financial support that came with the award allowed Bertha to carry on her activism. Her last major effort, made in 1912 when she was almost seventy, was a second lecture tour through the U.S. A year later, Bertha spoke at the International Peace Congress at The Hague, where she was honored for being "the generalissimo" of the peace movement, and for her lifelong dedication to peace.

Bertha died in June 1914, at the age of 71. She missed the outbreak of World War I by only a few weeks. Her final words were, "Lay down your arms! Tell it to all."

Jane Addams

Nobel Peace
Prize Laureate, 1931

America's "Leading Citizen"

Having integrity doesn't always make you popular. Because of her work on behalf of the poor, social reformer Jane Addams was one of the most loved women in the United States in the early 1900s. But Jane was also a pacifist, and her outspoken opposition to the United States joining World War I made her one of the most hated women in America.

Laura Jane Addams was born on September 6, 1860 in the rural village of Cedarville, Illinois. Sarah and John Addams were gentle, loving parents, but strict. Jane and

The Jane Addams Peace Association, together with the Women's International League for Peace and Freedom, give the annual Jane Addams Children's Book Awards to books that promote peace, equality, multiculturalism, and peaceful solutions.

her four older siblings—three others had died of cholera—were brought up in a serious, hard-working environment. When Jane was only two, her mother died in childbirth. Despite its tragic losses, the family was a happy one. The children lived in a beautiful house with a kind father who could afford a variety of comforts.

Jane was a frail and sensitive girl. She suffered from Pott's disease, a form of tuberculosis that caused a painfully curved spine. She didn't grow very tall and was self-conscious about her crooked posture. Although spoiled and pampered by her older siblings—and used to getting her own way—Jane learned strong values of generosity, compassion, and concern for others from her loving father.

John Addams owned the mill in Cedarville, and was a kind, respectful employer. He became a member of the Illinois State Legislature, where he served for sixteen years. A close friend of President Abraham Lincoln, and an abolitionist who spoke out against slavery, John was well-liked and respected for his generosity and integrity. He donated a library to Cedarville—he and Jane became its best customers—and the land for the community cemetery. Since John believed strongly in education, he also built a schoolhouse for the children of Cedarville.

Jane's father encouraged her to respect people's differences and to develop a strong work ethic. She described him as the "single cord" that "not only held fast my supreme affection, but also first drew me into the moral concerns of life." He was committed to a philosophy of charity, religious tolerance, and democracy.

Humility was also important to John, and this was a quality he tried to instill in his young daughter. One day, as she was proudly marching off to school in a beautiful new coat, her father stopped her. He wouldn't permit her to wear it because it might make the less-fortunate girls feel bad.

Jane became aware of extreme poverty at a young age. One day she and her father were riding through a poor section of a neighboring town. The smelly, noisy streets with shabby houses and ragged, hungry children shocked Jane, who had been sheltered in her comfortable home. She exclaimed that when she grew up, she would have "a large house, but it would not be built among the other large houses, but right in the midst of horrid little houses like these." Her prediction was surprisingly accurate.

When Jane was eight, her father married Anna Halderman, the children's piano teacher. Anna, who was sophisticated and cultured, worked hard to refine the atmosphere in the somewhat casual home. Jane's relationship with her new stepmother was polite but strained, and she resented her father's attention being taken away. She did learn from her stepmother's training, however; Jane developed an ease with the upper classes, which she used well in later years.

In 1877 it was still unusual for American girls to attend university or college. Nonetheless, John Addams encouraged his daughters to pursue higher learning, primarily because he believed that through education they would become better wives and mothers. Jane hoped to attend one of the new women's colleges that had recently opened, but her father was a trustee at nearby Rockford Female Seminary, so Jane and her older sisters went there.

Jane's marks were outstanding, and she became head

of the literary society, editor of the school magazine, school president, and valedictorian of her graduating class. Her classmates admired and respected her, and clamored to be her friend. Jane was reserved and serious, and—accustomed to intellectual conversations with her father—always ready for a friendly debate or discussion. But she didn't easily open her heart to friendship.

Ellen Gates Starr, a new student at Rockford during Jane's freshman year, found her way past Jane's reserve and quickly became her closest friend and constant companion. While they were alike in their intelligence and idealism, Jane and Ellen could not have been more different in their temperaments and academic endeavors. Sensitive and artistic Ellen studied literature and theater, while practical, earnest Jane pursued such subjects as science and sociology. Still, they spent much of their time at school together, and wrote long letters to each other when they were apart. They remained lifelong friends, and Ellen played a significant role in Jane's major achievements.

In 1881, Jane Addams graduated from Rockford, and a year later received her bachelor's degree from the newly designated Rockford College for Women. She planned to attend medical school—in an essay she had written in 1879, she claimed that women could become intelligent only "through the thorough study of at least one branch of physical science"—but her parents didn't approve. They were concerned that too much education would spoil Jane's chances to marry. Jane felt betrayed and frustrated. If her brothers could pursue studies in science and medicine, why couldn't she?

That same year, Jane's beloved father died of acute appendicitis. The town of Cedarville and all of Illinois grieved. Jane was devastated. In a letter to Ellen, Jane wrote, "The greatest sorrow that can ever come to me has passed, and I hope it is only a question of time until I get my moral pur-

poses straightened." It took years for Jane to recover, to sort out what direction her life was meant to take, and to understand how she could live up to her father's example.

Against her stepmother's wishes, Jane enrolled at the Women's Medical College of Philadelphia. Her studies were short-lived, however. Her heart

> "Nothing could be worse than the fear that one had given up too soon, and left one unexpended effort that might have saved the world."
>
> —Jane Addams

wasn't in it, and she was affected by her family's disapproval. As well, her health problems worsened, and in 1882 she required painful surgery. A back specialist told her family that she would probably not live another year. Her brother-in-law, himself a doctor, replied, "You don't know her. She'll outlive us all." The surgery was successful, but after the operation Jane had to lie on a board for six months, then wear an awkward brace of steel, leather, and whale-bone. She endured pain and discomfort for the rest of her life.

Jane's brother was meant to be in charge of managing the family's resources, but he suffered a mental breakdown. Only Jane was considered suitable to take up the task. The responsibility, coupled with her ongoing physical ailments and continued grief for her father, left Jane in a state of "nervous exhaustion." Her doctor recommended two years of travel, a common prescription then for rest and relaxation.

In the summer of 1883, Jane, her stepmother, and two friends from college set off for Europe. While Jane enjoyed many of the sights, she became frustrated with the extravagance of the travels and felt that her time was being wasted. However, one event stood as a signpost to Jane's future: she visited the slums at Mile End Road in East London. Jane was overwhelmed by the poverty, and "saw for the first time the overcrowded quarters of a great city at midnight." She was shocked by the crowds that begged and fought for the rotting food distributed at the Saturday food auction. Still, she didn't yet know what to do with the compassion this scene evoked.

When Jane returned home, she continued to struggle with physical pain and depression. She devoted herself to her family, but also found time for charity work. At twenty-seven, after years of fretting about how to live up to her father's example, Jane visited Europe again. Her old friend Ellen Starr accompanied her on this life-changing trip, which determined the course that both their lives would take.

When Jane and Ellen arrived in London, they were introduced to the founders of Toynbee Hall, a settlement house in the slums. The "Settlement Movement," which started in London, involved the creation of large communal homes— settlement houses—for poor people and immigrants in large cities. These houses offered food, shelter, and education, and were usually funded by wealthy donors. People involved in the movement actually lived—or "settled"—in the houses with the residents. Jane and Ellen were inspired by Toynbee Hall, and wanted to do similar work at home. For the first time since her father's death, Jane felt like she was regaining some of her moral purpose and direction.

Shortly after returning to the U.S., Jane and Ellen committed themselves to starting a settlement house in Chicago. Falling back on family acquaintances, the women started campaigning for donations. Money poured in. They found an old but well-kept mansion in a dirty and dilapidated part of town. They rented the place, named it Hull-House after the original owner, and on September 18, 1889, they moved in. Their first task was to encourage other well-off women from Chicago to share some of the responsibilities. Happily, they had no shortage of volunteers.

The hard work and dedication that Hull-House demanded were exactly what Jane's ailing spirit and body required. She moved out of her depression and was energized by her efforts and the stimulating demands of the project.

> "I do not believe that women are better than men. We have not wrecked railroads, nor corrupted legislature, nor done many unholy things that men have done; but then we must remember that we have not had the chance."
> —Jane Addams

Jane's goal with Hull-House was to balance inequalities between people—not just the rich and the poor, but also people of different racial and cultural backgrounds. She hoped the residents would recognize the things they had in common as well as the qualities that made them unique. She wanted to share her belief that the "things that make men like are finer and better than the things that keep them apart."

Many of the people who lived at or visited Hull-House were poor immigrants from Italy, Russia, Poland, Germany, Ireland, and Greece. Hull-House provided a kindergarten and day care center for the children, as well as a community kitchen and health care from visiting nurses. It became a meeting place for clubs and labor unions, and a refuge for lonely seniors. Within a few years, Hull-House provided legal aid and offered classes in English, vocational skills, music, art, and theater.

One day in 1890, a woman named Mary Rozet Smith, the daughter of a wealthy paper manufacturer, arrived at Hull-House. She became Jane's devoted companion, tending to her when she was ill, handling her social correspondence, and making her travel arrangements. Mary's own large home became a place of refuge for Jane when life at the settlement house weighed her down. In letters, Jane affectionately refers to herself and Mary as "married." Over the years, Mary also became the single biggest financial contributor to Hull-House.

Hull-House grew to include the Butler Art Gallery, the Hull-House Labor Museum, a gymnasium, a swimming pool, a clubhouse for girls, a book bindery, an art studio, a library, and an employment bureau. By 1910, up to seventy people lived in Hull-House and more than two thousand people entered each day. Jane and Ellen's dreams of bringing the rich and poor together in one community had come true, as had Jane's childhood prediction to her father that she would live in a grand house among the poor.

Halvdan Koht, a member of the Nobel Committee, visited Jane at Hull-House. He said later, "When you meet Miss Addams [at Hull-House] . . . you immediately become poignantly aware that she has built a home and in it is a mother to one and all. She is not one to talk much, but her quiet, great-hearted personality inspires confidence and creates an atmosphere of goodwill which instinctively brings out the best in everyone." The success of Hull-House inspired others, and six years after Hull-House opened, there were more than twenty settlement houses across the country.

Through her work at Hull-House, Jane Addams came to understand that meaningful social change could only come about through government and legislative reform. She had succeeded in improving the lives of people in one neighbourhood in Chicago, and now wanted to apply this work more broadly. Women had not yet won the vote (Jane was the first vice-president of the National American Woman Suffrage Association), but Jane believed that women must make their voices heard in government.

These were busy years for Jane. She focused her efforts on the causes of poverty, lobbying the state to examine laws governing labor and the juvenile justice system. She worked for legislation to protect immigrants from exploitation, limit working hours for women, make school mandatory for children, support labor unions, and provide safe workplaces. Jane was particularly concerned about the protection of children's rights. She thought it was unfair for adolescents to be tried in adult court, and so worked on the development of a juvenile court system. The first juvenile court in the world opened in 1899 in Chicago.

Reflecting the spirit of tolerance and equality that she had learned from her father, she was a charter member of the National Association for the Advancement of Colored People and a founding member of the American Civil Liberties Union.

She published eleven books and numerous articles, and maintained an active speaking schedule across the country and around the world. She was cheered and adored wherever she traveled, and people across the globe were grateful for her commitment to improving the lives of women, children, workers, and immigrants. She placed second behind inventor Thomas Edison in a 1913 newspaper poll that asked, "Who among our contemporaries are of the most value to our community?"

When World War I broke out in 1914, Jane and a group of women pacifists began to organize and make connections with the international peace movement, in hopes of keeping the U.S. out of the war. On January 10, 1915, more than three thousand women attended a meeting in the ballroom of the New Willard Hotel in Washington, DC. This was the launch of the Woman's Peace Party; Jane Addams was elected chair.

The proclamation of the Woman's Peace Party read: "We women of the United States, assembled in behalf of World Peace, grateful for the security of our own country, but sorrowing for the misery of all involved in the present struggle among warring nations, do hereby band ourselves together to demand that war be abolished . . . We demand that women be given a share in deciding between war and peace in all the courts of high debate—within the home, the school, the church, the industrial order and the state."

In April 1915, a suffragist group in Holland invited members of the Woman's Peace Party to an International Congress of Women in The Hague. Jane was asked to chair this meeting of more than thirteen hundred women from Europe and North America who came together to protest against the war in Europe.

Back in America, however, these peace-loving women were attacked in the press and in hostile letters from people who felt that they were disloyal to their country and meddling in men's affairs. U.S. President Theodore Roosevelt, who had been a friend and supporter of Jane and of Hull-House, described them as "hysterical pacifists," and said that "poor bleeding Jane" had become "one of the shrieking sisterhood." Jane was expelled from the Daughters of the American Revolution, who had recently made her an honorary member, and she was accused of being a socialist, a communist, a traitor, and a fool. FBI Director J. Edgar Hoover called her "the most dangerous woman in America." The U.S. joined the war in 1917, and the attacks against Jane continued.

Jane Addams, in black at center, gives a speech to a crowd.

Jane was not deterred. She was elected first president of the newly formed Women's International League for Peace and Freedom (WILPF), and she maintained her role as spokesperson for pacifist women until her death. Jane also persevered at Hull-House, which continued to serve its community in Chicago. When the Depression of the 1930s struck, Hull-House and other settlement houses became more necessary than ever. Eventually, criticism shifted back to praise, and Jane regained her place of honor in the minds of Americans.

In 1931, Jane Addams was awarded the Nobel Peace Prize. In his presentation, Halvdan Koht said of Jane, "Little by little, through no attempt to draw attention by her work but simply through the patient self-sacrifice and quiet ardor which she devoted to [peace], she won an eminent place in the love and esteem of her people. She became the leading woman in the nation, one might almost say its leading citizen."

Jane, who had suffered with physical ailments throughout her life, had a heart attack in 1926. She never fully regained her health. On December 10, 1931, as the Nobel Peace Prize was being awarded to her in Oslo, Jane was being admitted to a Baltimore hospital. She died a few years later, on May 21, 1935. The funeral was held in the courtyard of Hull-House. More than two thousand people an hour came to pay their respects. She was buried with her father in the family plot in Cedarville, near her childhood home.

Emily Greene Balch

Nobel Peace
Prize Laureate, 1946

"A Warm Personal Desire to Serve the Common Good"

Emily Greene Balch was born in Jamaica Plain, a prosperous Boston suburb, on January 8, 1867. Remembering her privileged childhood, she said, "Mine was a simple, happy, suburban home. Grass underfoot and a sky overhead were part of my birthright. It was a shock to me when I . . . realized many children have never spent a night in the dark, have never spent a night in silence."

Emily's family was not just well off; it was also large and loving. She had four sisters and one brother, and was surrounded by grandparents, aunts, uncles, and cousins.

Still, Emily felt concern for those who weren't as lucky as she was and, as she grew older, she fiercely defended the rights of women, immigrants, and the poor. She became a social worker, then a teacher, and finally a full-time activist for peace.

The seeds of Emily's ability to think beyond herself were planted by her parents. Ellen Noyes and Francis V. Balch belonged to the Unitarian church and believed strongly in freedom of thought and respect for other religious traditions. They raised their children with high moral and religious standards, and with a commitment to social responsibility. Her father was a respected lawyer committed to civil liberties, and from him she learned the importance of "complete acceptance of the role of conscience and . . . a warm and generous sense of the call to service." Her parents' friends were opponents of slavery, and members of Emily's family were community leaders who fought for religious tolerance.

In many ways, Emily's childhood was blissfully ordinary. She was an active, playful girl, who enjoyed nature and climbing trees, and—especially when she received her first prescription for eyeglasses when she was ten years old—she loved reading. She particularly enjoyed stories about young girls who became heroines with important missions. She attended private schools, and at age thirteen went to Miss Ireland's School in Boston where she focused on languages and literature.

At the same time, Emily's extraordinary commitment to justice continued to grow. As a girl, she was strongly influenced by Unitarian minister Charles Fletcher Dole. She remembered that, "he asked us to enlist in the service of goodness, and to meet the demands of this service whatever its cost. In accepting this pledge . . . I consciously dedicated myself as genuinely as a nun taking her vows, and in spite of endless weakness, wrongdoings, blunders, and failures, I think I never abandoned in any way my desire to live up to it."

Tragedy struck the Balch family when Emily was seventeen. Her mother died, and Emily was devastated. Her father decided she should travel to Europe to recover and sent her away accompanied by a family friend. Along with cathedrals and museums, Emily was exposed to a variety of cultures. But she also witnessed the effects of poverty. This poverty stunned her and she redoubled her commitment to economic fairness.

In 1886, Emily returned from Europe and entered Bryn Mawr, a newly founded college for women. She began studying literature and classics, but her desire to improve the lot of the poor made her want to explore how money affects society. She switched to economics in her senior year, feeling that literature was "an indulgence" and that "this was no time for 'idle singers of an empty day' but for efforts to study and better conditions." She was a member of the college's first graduating class in 1889 and was awarded the first Bryn Mawr European Fellowship, which allowed her to spend a year in Paris studying with Émile Levasseur, a famous economist. The recommendation from the college read, "She is twenty-two years of age, a woman of unusual ability, of extraordinary beauty, of moral character, of great discretion and balance of judgment, very unselfish, and in every way fit to be a representative of the College and to engage in study in Europe."

Emily was an intelligent and well-liked student. A friend in Paris described her as "a tall, slim girl in her early twenties . . . with a magnificent smooth forehead, and gleaming young hair . . . Her great eyes were clear, intelligent, calm, as few eyes ever are. She dressed simply and unobtrusively . . . The whole school was proud to have her there . . . She was called 'The Intellectual'."

While in Paris, Emily researched and wrote *Public Assistance of the Poor in France*, her first book and the first expression of her interest in social work and working with the impoverished and disadvantaged. She was eager to return to the U.S. and put her knowledge to work in her home country.

When Emily arrived in Boston, she began working with children in the slums. She contributed her skills to a children's library program, served on the boards of a children's home and at the Children's Aid Society, and developed a manual on juvenile delinquency.

Emily's activism was marked by both practicality and intellectual curiosity. In the summer of 1892, she attended the School for Applied Ethics in Plymouth, Massachusetts. She took part in a program designed for settlement house workers, and met other reform-minded women, including Jane Addams, who had started Chicago's Hull-House, the first settlement house in the United States. Jane and Emily became lifelong friends and—in later years—companions in the peace movement.

In December of 1892, Jane and Emily co-founded Denison House, a small settlement house in Boston, which served as a meeting place for young women who worked in the tobacco, laundry, or garment industries. Denison House also became a refuge for prostitutes, abused women, the homeless, abandoned children, labor activists, and other needy people from the streets of Boston. For the first few years, Emily worked full-time at Denison House, teaching and serving its residents and clients.

During the early 1890s, Emily also continued her university studies, taking sociology courses at Harvard and the University of Chicago. In 1895, she studied economics at the University of Berlin.

A chance encounter on the ship coming back from

Europe changed her life. Sailing toward home, Emily was intending to complete her Ph.D. But onboard, she ran into an old friend, Katherine Coman, who had become the sole economics professor at Wellesley College. Katherine convinced Emily to apply for a teaching position, and soon Emily was a professor at Wellesley, teaching courses on economics, sociology, the labor movement, and the history of socialism.

"The soldiers in the hospitals say to their nurses: 'We don't know why we are fighting. Can't you women help us?' That is the very question we are trying to answer."
—Emily Greene Balch, concluding her report to the International Congress of Women at the Hague, May 1915

A gifted and enthusiastic instructor, she organized the first undergraduate courses in the country on social work and immigration. Committed to action as well as theory, and in hopes of developing compassion and a sense of duty in her students, Emily made field trips and volunteering a regular part of her curriculum. She led her students to prisons, through slums, to asylums for the mentally ill, and of course to Denison House. Her students respected her and were impressed by her imaginative thinking, wide-ranging experiences, and compassion. In 1913, Emily was appointed Chair of Political Economy and Political and Social Science at Wellesley, a significant recognition of her intelligence and talent, and an enormous achievement for a woman of that time.

Not content to rest in the luxury of her newfound status, Emily tirelessly continued her activism. Besides teaching at Wellesley and spending time at Denison House, she became active in the movements for women's suffrage, racial justice, and the control of child labor. In 1902, she became president

In 1955, concerned about poor relations between the United States and China, Emily wrote a poem—a "letter of love" to the "Dear People of China." This is the final stanza:

"Let us be patient with one another,
And even patient with ourselves.
We have a long, long way to go.
So let us hasten along the road,
The road of human tenderness and generosity.
Groping, we may find one another's hands in the dark."

of the Women's Trade Union League of Boston, which she co-founded. She also chaired the Minimum Wage Committee, which successfully advocated for the first minimum-wage law in the U.S.

At a time when many Americans were fearful of the waves of European immigrants flooding into the country, Emily took a strong interest in these often vulnerable people. She studied the immigrant communities, spoke out on their behalf, and tried to help her fellow Americans understand the immigrant experience. She researched and wrote *Our Slavic Fellow Citizens*, a study of immigrants from Czechoslovakia and Austria-Hungary. While researching the book, Emily visited most of the Slavic communities in the U.S., and in 1905 she took a year off from Wellesley and traveled to Austria-Hungary. She wanted to live among the people she was researching, and to study their conditions firsthand.

As the threat of war loomed, Emily's attention was drawn toward the peace movement. She closely followed the two international peace conferences at The Hague in 1899 and 1907, and after the outbreak of World War I in Europe in 1914, Emily was determined to work for peace. The United States had not yet entered the war and Emily hoped her country would stay out of it.

She requested a leave of absence from Wellesley to pursue her pacifist activities and became a delegate to the International Congress of Women at The Hague in 1915. She played a prominent role in several important projects, including co-founding the organization that became the Women's International League for Peace and Freedom (WILPF). Through WILPF, Emily and her companions mobilized women to act to keep the U.S. out of the war. Emily met directly with President Woodrow Wilson and, in one three-day period—before the days of text messages and e-mail—WILPF organized American women to send 12,000 anti-war telegrams to the White House.

Emily extended her leave from Wellesley. She wrote *Approaches to the*

Thousands of American women and the organizations they belonged to had argued against U.S. involvement in World War I. The U.S. War Department felt that it was necessary to keep these members of "The Socialist-Pacifist Movement in America" under surveillance. In 1923, a War Department librarian published the "Spider Web Chart," a document with lines showing the connections between prominent women and the organizations with which they were associated, along with summaries of their "radical" views. The chart was used to defeat bills and resolutions proposed by women's groups throughout the 1920s, and to threaten the organizations and to accuse the women of disloyalty to their country. In addition to Emily and WILPF, the chart included the PTA, the YWCA, the Children's Bureau, the General Federation of Women's Clubs, and the Women's Christian Temperance Union.

Great Settlement, a book that offered various proposals for peaceful reconciliation. Despite the efforts of the American peace movement, the U.S. entered World War I in 1917.

With American soldiers fighting in Europe, public opinion shifted against the protesters. In 1919, Emily asked again to extend her leave of absence but because of her controversial and outspoken views, Wellesley terminated her contract instead. At fifty-two years old, Emily was forced to give up teaching, which she loved, as well as her pension and a prestigious position at one of the country's most respected colleges.

She responded by working even harder in the pacifist cause. She joined the Woman's Peace Party and attended the second convention of the International Congress of Women held in Zurich, Switzerland in 1919. She became secretary-treasurer of WILPF—Jane Addams was its president—and spent the next four years traveling across Europe and the U.S. studying and speaking out on behalf of the peace movement. She dedicated the next twenty years of her life to pacifism.

Emily's life was defined not by a single courageous act, but by a lifelong dedication to her moral principles, which played out in many areas, and which were informed by her Unitarian faith. In 1921, she took the next step in her spiritual journey and became a Quaker. The Religious Society of Friends, whose members are known as Quakers, is a Christian organization that emphasizes human goodness and believes that God exists in everyone. Among other things, Quakers believe in equality between women and men. They also believe strongly in non-violence. Now, as then, many conscientious objectors and anti-war activists are Quakers. In the Society of Friends, Emily found a community that, like her, was dedicated to a combination of activism and spirituality.

Because of failing health, Emily resigned from WILPF in

1922, but she continued to volunteer, research, speak, and study. Her lifetime of service began to be celebrated, even by the college that had rejected her. In 1935, Wellesley College invited Emily to deliver their Armistice Day Address, a satisfying resolution to the abrupt end of her teaching career there sixteen years earlier. And ten years later, it was the President of Wellesley, Mildred McAfee Horton, who sponsored the campaign to nominate Emily for the Nobel Peace Prize.

In 1946, when she was seventy-nine years old, Emily was honored with that award. In her Nobel lecture, which she titled "Toward Human Unity or Beyond Nationalism," she expressed her view that, despite the evidence around them, peace was still possible. She said, "We are not asked to subscribe to any utopia or to believe in a perfect world just around the corner. We are asked to be patient with necessarily slow and groping advance on the road forward, and to be ready for each step ahead as it becomes practicable. We are asked to equip ourselves with courage, hope, readiness for hard work, and to cherish large and generous ideals." Emily turned over most of her Nobel prize money to WILPF, and became its honorary chair.

When she was eighty-eight years old, Emily received the American Unitarian Association Award for her devotion to "a lifetime . . . crusading for civil liberties, interracial brotherhood, social and civic righteousness, and world peace." In her acceptance speech, she expressed her faith in a better world: "The time has come to break down the dikes and let the healing waters flow over us. I see in us, young and old, the seed of the world that is to be."

After a lifetime of working for others, Emily died on January 9, 1961, one day after her ninety-fourth birthday.

Betty Williams and Máiread Corrigan Maguire

Nobel Peace
Prize Laureates, 1976

"The Peace People"

It was a warm summer day in Belfast, the capital of Northern Ireland, when Betty Williams heard gunshots, followed by the crash of a car smashing into a fence. She ran to investigate and met a horrifying scene. Danny Lennon, a nineteen-year-old Irish Republican Army (IRA) gunman, had been shot dead while trying to escape British soldiers. His out-of-control car slammed into a woman and her three young children. Eight-year-old Joanne and six-week-old Andrew were killed instantly. Their two-year-old brother, John, died the next day. Their mother, Anne Maguire, was seriously injured with

"I am angry, the Peace People are angry that war at home dribbles on, and around the world we see the same stupidity gathering momentum for far worse wars than the little one which the little population of Northern Ireland has had to endure. We are angry at the waste of resources that goes on everyday for militarism while human beings live in misery."

—Betty Williams, from her Nobel Peace Prize acceptance speech

two broken legs and a broken pelvis.

Anne Maguire's sister, Máiread Corrigan, had just returned from a holiday that day, August 10th, 1976. She received the tragic news and then accompanied her grief-stricken brother-in-law to the hospital to identify his dead children, her niece and nephew.

Living in Northern Ireland, Betty and Máiread were part of a population that had been wracked by unspeakable violence for more than a century. Because they were both Roman Catholic, they were on the same side of a struggle that pitted the Protestant majority against the Catholic minority in a fierce political fight.

Officially, Northern Ireland was, and still is, a part of the United Kingdom (together with England, Scotland, and Wales). However, many people, most of whom were Catholic, believed that Northern Ireland should be reunited with Ireland to form one country, the Republic of Ireland. These people were called "Nationalists" or "Republicans." Those in favor of strengthening ties with Britain were called "Unionists," and were mostly members of the Protestant majority.

Tensions between the Catholic minority and the Protestant majority were strong, and each waged war against the other. Pro-Nationalist groups such as the IRA and Sinn Fein battled with pro-Unionist groups—the Ulster Volunteer

Force and the British military. During "the Troubles," the name commonly used for this period of devastating violence, the streets of Belfast were filled with tanks and soldiers. Throughout the worst years, from 1969 to 1998, many thousands of people were killed in brutal attacks and random bombings. Quiet neighborhoods became war zones and innocent people—often children—were the victims.

After accompanying her brother-in-law to the hospital, Máiread Corrigan went to the local television studio and made an emotional, on-air appeal for an end to the horror. "It's not violence that people want," she cried. Betty Williams watched Máiread make her courageous plea on the news that night, a plea that was broadcast across Northern Ireland and around the world.

Although Betty had been living amidst the Troubles for many years, she was shaken by the senseless deaths of the children and the teenaged driver, and overwhelmed by her need to do something. Acting purely on intuition, Betty started talking to her neighbors. "Do you want to have peace?" she asked. Betty received a passionate response. Within two days she had gathered more than six thousand signatures on a petition demanding an end to the senseless bloodshed in their community.

The actions of Máiread and Betty released an outpouring of grief. Throughout Belfast, chapels were packed for prayers and groups of people gathered at the death site to pray for the dead children and their family. Forty-eight hours after the accident, Betty herself spoke on a local TV station and read out the text of her petition. She declared, "I don't know if we are going to succeed in our campaign for peace, but I can assure you that we are going to do our very best." She courageously called on Protestant women to unite with Catholic women in the name of peace.

Máiread called Betty to thank her for her support, and

asked her to attend the children's funeral the next day. Thousands showed up to follow the hearse with the three small, white coffins to the graveyard. Betty and Máiread met in person for the first time, and started to make plans for a peace march.

The following day, only four days after the tragedy, more than ten thousand women walked side by side through the streets of Belfast to the graves of the three young siblings. Betty and Máiread were overwhelmed by the support from women young and old, rich and poor, Catholic and Protestant—and astonished at their courage. Just by showing up, these women were putting themselves at risk from both Nationalist and Unionist supporters, and they were ridiculed and assaulted along the way. A crowd of angry teenagers threw rocks and bottles, and a group of Protestant women in particular was brutally attacked. They were called names—"traitors" and "whores"—and had nothing to protect themselves with except their umbrellas. But the bruised and bloodied women, who continued to march and sing hymns, found strength in their numbers and remained united in their singular message: "Enough!"

The march was an historic moment for Northern Ireland. This was the first time that Belfast, which had been immersed in bloodshed for decades, had witnessed such an enormous outcry for peace. As Betty described it, "A deep sense of frustration at the mindless stupidity of the continuing violence was already evident before the tragic events of that sunny afternoon of August 10, 1976. But the deaths of those four young people in one terrible moment of violence caused that frustration to explode, and create the possibility of a real peace movement."

A week after this first march, Máiread and Betty formed an organization called Women for Peace. They led another march through the streets of Belfast, this time with more than thirty-five thousand supporters. They still had no strategy and no clear goals beyond stopping the violence, but they knew they needed to continue what they had started.

Máiread and Betty were joined by Ciaran McKeown, a sympathetic newspaper reporter who wanted to help build this grassroots movement. He had been covering the Troubles in Belfast for many years, and was moved and excited by what was happening. Women for Peace became The Community of Peace People, and then simply Peace People, an organization with the goals of encouraging the end

"My mother has been my greatest supporter for peace. One time we were in the U.S. protesting against nuclear weapons and I was put in jail overnight. I returned home to Ireland and my mother asked, 'Why did you stay just one night? We need to get rid of those weapons!'"
—Máiread Corrigan Maguire

of fighting in Northern Ireland and providing services for the victims of violence. They organized weekly marches across the United Kingdom. Many thousands of people who had also decided that they'd had enough joined them. Solidarity demonstrations took place all over the world, inspired by Máiread and Betty's courage.

But they didn't just organize marches. Máiread and Betty spoke out publicly against the IRA and other paramilitary groups that had participated in the violence. They spoke to both Catholics and Protestants, Nationalists and Unionists. This alone was an act of great courage. They spoke out against the British government and fearlessly stood up for human rights, peace, and non-violence. Looking back on that time, Betty said, "We are for life and creation, and we are against war and destruction, and in our rage in that terrible week we screamed that the violence had to stop."

Máiread Corrigan Maguire (top) and Betty Williams (bottom)

Not everyone embraced this new movement for peace. Critics ridiculed the women and called them naïve. "We were seen as betraying our communities, no matter what side we came from, but we really were not against one side or another," Máiread explained. Both Máiread and Betty received death threats and hate mail, and more than once barely escaped serious injury. After one protest, Máiread's car was torched. "Betty is a Traitor" was painted on the walls in Betty's neighborhood. Years later, Máiread recalled, "We went in at a rather emotional time, perhaps unwisely, but in those days we often did unwise things."

Máiread and Betty continued, supported by Ciaran's expertise. He said, "We have to do things that people don't expect us to do. We have to be stronger and braver than anyone else, including the paramilitary organizations." With Ciaran's help, they wrote the "Declaration of the Peace People," a simple document that they used to challenge people in Northern Ireland and around the world to dedicate themselves to peace and non-violence. It states:

"We have a simple message for the world from this movement for Peace. We want to live and love and build a just and peaceful society. We want for our children, as we want for ourselves, our lives at home, at work, and at play to be lives of joy and Peace. We recognize that to build such a society demands dedication, hard work, and courage. We recognize that there are many problems in our society which are a source of conflict and violence. We recognize that every bullet fired and every exploding bomb make that work more difficult. We reject the use of the bomb and the bullet and all the techniques of violence. We dedicate ourselves to working with our neighbours, near and far, day in and day out, to build that peaceful society in which the tragedies we have known are a bad memory and a continuing warning."

In October of 1977, Máiread and Betty were honored with the Nobel Peace Prize for 1976. Receiving the Peace Prize greatly increased the media and public attention that Máiread's and Betty's campaign received. Belfast was paying attention, and the rest of the world was now watching, too. By the end of 1977, more than 100,000 people in Northern Ireland had signed the Declaration. It took twenty more years of negotiations—and twenty more years of violence and killing—for a settlement to be reached and for a cautious peace to be declared in Northern Ireland. But the Peace People campaign was the first step.

It's not surprising that a grassroots peace movement would emerge from the mayhem of the Troubles. It is fascinating, however, that two quiet, "ordinary" women—both office workers and housewives—would lead the charge.

Elizabeth (Betty) Smyth was born in Belfast in May, 1943. Her Protestant father was a butcher and her Catholic mother, a housewife. When Betty was thirteen, her mother was paralyzed by a stroke. Young Betty took on the enormous responsibility of caring for her mother, as well as for her younger sister. Betty attended Catholic schools until she graduated, and then took a two-year secretarial course. She started working as a receptionist and, at eighteen, married Ralph Williams, a Protestant like her father.

When she started Peace People, Betty Williams was thirty-four and had no background in peacemaking or activism. She was working as a receptionist and raising her two young children, and there was little about her life that would prepare her for the demands and challenges of being an activist and Nobel Peace Laureate.

Betty's life had been touched directly by the violence in Northern Ireland—she had lost two cousins in the conflict. But speaking of the years before Peace People, Betty said, "I really did nothing for peace or for reconciling the two communities. I was one of the apathetic ones. I belonged to the silent majority. I always wanted to do something, but I couldn't decide what it was that I should do." The events of August 1976 changed all of that.

Máiread (pronounced mu-RADE—it's Irish for Margaret) Corrigan was also born in Belfast, a few months after Betty, in January, 1944. She is the second of seven children in a Roman Catholic family. She had inherited a strong faith from her mother, and attended Catholic schools until she turned fourteen. After one year at Miss Gordon's Commercial College, her parents could no longer afford to pay the Catholic school tuition, so Máiread quit school. She joined The Legion of Mary, an organization that did volunteer work with prisoners and children with disabilities. She dedicated herself to this for many years, even after she began working full-time. Growing up Catholic in Belfast, Máiread had learned to hate the British soldiers, and had even considered joining the IRA. At age sixteen, she took a job as a secretary and did secretarial work until that 1976 summer day, when her world, like Betty's, was irrevocably changed.

Receiving the Nobel Peace Prize was startling for these

"The voice of women, the voice of those most closely involved in bringing forth new life, has not always been listened to when it pleaded and implored against the waste of life in war after war. The voice of women has a special role and a special soul force in the struggle for a nonviolent world."
—Betty Williams, from her Nobel Peace Prize acceptance speech

45

unassuming women. Years later, Máiread recalled, "The greatest difficulty I had was facing university professors and intellectuals and people like that. That was a greater challenge than living in my community, whose emotions I understood." And Betty humbly remembered, "I really [didn't] like the VIP treatment. I prefer to stand in line with everyone else than go to the head of the line—all because I'm Betty Williams who had the nerve to say it was wrong to kill people."

Máiread and Betty remain committed to a world without violence, and to breaking down the barriers that separate people and allow war to exist. And they have both expanded their efforts for peace beyond the boundaries of Northern Ireland.

Betty and Máiread (far right) with the other Nobel Peace Prize Laureates who founded the Nobel Women's Initiative, Wangari Maathai, Jody Williams, and Shirin Ebadi.

Betty left the Peace People, and in 1982 she left Northern Ireland for the United States, where she continued to work and speak out for peace, human rights, and the nonviolent struggle for justice. She is now President of the World Centers of Compassion for Children International (WCCCI), which she founded in 1997. She has traveled the world to speak about what she describes as the "injustices, cruelty and horror perpetrated on the world's children."

Betty has received many awards. The popular Canadian rock band Nickelback even honored her with their hit song and video "If Everyone Cared." In 2004, Betty returned to her home in Belfast, where she still lives.

In 1980, Máiread's sister Anne committed suicide. She had never recovered from the deaths of her three children. Máiread helped her widowed brother-in-law with his three remaining children, and a couple of years later they married.

Máiread, now Máiread Corrigan Maguire, continues to work with the Peace People, and has expanded the organization's reach beyond Northern Ireland. A devout Catholic, Máiread is a member of the International Peace Council and has become a leader in the International Fellowship of Reconciliation, the world's oldest interfaith pacifist organization. She has supported the ordination of women to the priesthood in the Catholic Church and has called for Catholic leaders to speak out for justice and peace. She has also become active in the anti-nuclear movement and she often speaks against nuclear weapons. In a recent article, she wrote, "I believe we all have a human right to a nuclear-free world and, in proclaiming that right, we affirm that we have chosen to live together, as the human family and friends, and not to die together as fools in a nuclear holocaust."

Both Betty and Máiread are co-founders of the Nobel Women's Initiative and have been involved in its activities on behalf of human rights and peace.

Not all Nobel Peace Laureates set out to change the world. Sometimes good people react to horrible events with such strength and tenacity, and with such startling vision, that they surprise even themselves. Neither Betty nor Máiread had a history in pacifism, social justice, or in the theory and practice of nonviolence. In his presentation speech, Egil Aarvik said, "There was no talk here of ingenious theories, or shrewd diplomacy or pompous declarations. No, their contribution was a far better one: a courageous, unselfish act that proved an inspiration to thousands, that lit a light in the darkness, and that gave fresh hope to people who believed that all hope was gone."

Mother Teresa

Nobel Peace
Prize Laureate, 1979

"A Pencil in God's Hand"

Mother Teresa is one of the most famous religious figures of our time. But her spiritual life wasn't easy. Working with the poor, the wretched, and the dying in the slums of India, she sometimes felt that God was ignoring her pleas for guidance. Nonetheless, she continued her labor, filling the gaps in her certainty with something else: determination.

Mother Teresa's faith was firmly planted in her childhood. She was born Agnes Gonxha Bojaxhiu on August 26, 1910, in Skopje, a town that was then in the Ottoman Empire, but is now in Macedonia in southeastern Europe. Her family

> "There is a terrible hunger for love. We all experience that in our lives—the pain, the loneliness. We must have the courage to recognize it. The poor may be right in your own family. Find them. Love them."
> —Mother Teresa

was part of the small Roman Catholic minority that existed within the Muslim majority.

Her father, Nikola, was a successful merchant who died when Agnes was nine. Some accounts say that he succumbed to illness, while others say he was poisoned for his support of Albanian nationalism. Before Nikola's death, the family had lived comfortably in a large house with gardens and fruit trees, but after his passing they were left with little.

Agnes's mother, Drana, was a strong woman who responded to her widowhood by exhibiting three qualities that her daughter would become famous for: tenacity, faith, and generosity. She started an embroidery business and managed to raise her children on her earnings. She was also a devout Roman Catholic and set an example of charity for young Agnes by taking individuals who were even less fortunate then she was into her home. Mother Teresa's constant reference to Jesus' words: "I was hungry and you gave me to eat; I was thirsty and you gave me to drink; I was homeless and you took me in," reflects her mother's influence on her life.

Not surprisingly for someone who is often referred to as a saint, Agnes was a well-behaved girl. Her brother, Lazar, remembers that once, when they were supposed to be fasting before Mass, he tried to talk her into raiding the jelly cupboard with him. Agnes refused and gave him a good scolding. She never did tell on him, though.

As she grew up, faith—and her struggles with it—became

the center of Agnes's life. Agnes was only twelve when she first felt a calling to become a nun. But doubt arose alongside her strong faith and made her ask how she knew her calling was real. She turned to her local priest, who told her to look for the presence of joy when she contemplated becoming a nun. The priest said, "Joy that comes from the depths of your being is like a compass by which you can tell what direction your life should follow. That is the case even when the road you must take is a difficult one."

". . . it is important that everyone is seen as equal before God. I've always said we should help a Hindu become a better Hindu, a Muslim become a better Muslim, a Catholic become a better Catholic. We believe our work should be our example to people."
—Mother Teresa

Agnes didn't immediately know what direction to take, but her desire to lead a religious life grew stronger when she was a teenager, especially when she heard letters from missionaries read out in church. Their enthusiastic descriptions of their work in India, and especially of the children there, helped to convince Agnes that she should commit herself to a religious life.

But what order of nuns should she join? There are many different societies of nuns who exercise their faith in different ways. Agnes had heard about a group of Irish nuns who worked in India as teachers. The Loreto Sisters had been missionaries in India since the 1840s, and for their time they were quite progressive; they worked hard to educate women in communities where education for women was not particularly valued.

Agnes decided that this was her chance. At eighteen, she took the long train ride to England and then crossed the Irish Channel by boat to become a novitiate—a beginning nun—at the Loreto Abbey in Rathfarnan, Ireland. This journey must have been exciting for a young girl from Albania, but Agnes never saw her sister or her beloved mother again.

After only six weeks in Rathfaran, Agnes was sent to Darjeeling, near the Himalayan mountains in India, to study for two years. On the way to Darjeeling, Agnes stopped over in the vast and crowded city of Calcutta. As she left the train station and walked past the open sewers and shanties of the city, she was shocked by the poverty she saw. The hot, steamy streets were filled with crowds of people moving in all directions. Rickshaws passed by her, narrowly missing corpses left on the side of the road, and people everywhere were begging for food. She knew that she had come to India to bring comfort to those in need, but the immensity of the need must have been staggering.

When she got to the Lareto Convent in Darjeeling, Agnes studied religious subjects as well as Hindi, Bengali, and English, which was the language used in missionary schools. She also prepared to teach geography. During this time, she wore the traditional black habit and was "cloistered," which means that she was enclosed in a convent, away from the world.

Agnes took her "first vows" as a nun in 1931, and her final "solemn vows" on May 14, 1937. From that day on, she became known as Sister Teresa. Selecting a name is a meaningful step. Thérèse de Lisieux, the French Carmelite nun after whom Agnes named herself, is the patron saint of missionaries.

From 1931 to 1948, she worked as a teacher at St. Mary's High School in Calcutta, eventually becoming its Principal or Mother Superior. Her life at St. Mary's Convent was generally one of comfort; she taught geography to daughters of wealthy European and Indian families. Teresa—now known as Mother Teresa—enjoyed teaching and, although she could be demanding, she was also known for her quick wit and laughter. One of her fellow nuns said, "In those early years, there was nothing to suggest that she would ever leave Loreto, nothing at all."

As happy as Mother Teresa was, the world outside the convent school must have been a temptation for a nun whose real desire was to work directly with the suffering. A famine in India in 1943 brought misery and death. As well, India was on the verge of independence from British rule, and rioting broke out between Muslims and Hindus. Thousands of people lost their lives and thousands more were injured or left homeless.

During the rioting, the school became a place of refuge for more than three hundred of St. Mary's students. At one point, Mother Teresa bravely snuck out of the convent to find food for them. The scene of destruction she met was overwhelming. Bodies lay abandoned in the streets; shops were burned; vultures circled; and smoke from funeral pyres rose from every direction.

During this volatile period, Mother Teresa fell ill and was sent to recuperate in the Himalayan foothills. This journey changed her life. While traveling to the foothills by train on September 10th, 1946, she received her second "calling." This was "an inner command," she said, "to renounce Loreto, where I was very happy, to go to serve the poor in the streets . . . It was an order . . . I felt God wanted something more from me." September 10th became known by her followers as "Inspiration Day."

In the spring of 1948, Mother Teresa was given permission by her superiors to live and work in the Calcutta slums while still keeping her vows as a nun. She replaced her traditional Loreto habit for an Indian dress called a sari. The sari she chose was made of white cotton with a blue edge, and covered her head as well as her body.

Slums are run-down areas of a city where the poorest people live. Slum buildings, made from flimsy materials, can be simple shacks or huge permanent settlements. Most slums lack underground sewage, electricity and clean water. In Kolkata (formerly Calcutta), in 1991, over thirty percent of the twelve million inhabitants were living in slums. That's 3.6 million people!

Committing herself to her new life, Mother Teresa took an intensive nursing course, became an Indian citizen, and rented a room in the slums. She had almost no teaching materials. In the first weeks, she gathered children under a tree and used the mud floor as a blackboard. Using sticks, she scratched out letters on the ground. Because she was concerned about her students' health as well as their education, she encouraged them by giving them milk and bars of soap.

Mother Teresa wrote in her diary that the first year was extremely difficult. She had no income and often had to beg for food and supplies. She felt lonely and often thought about returning to the comfort of convent life, but she gained a deep appreciation for the lives of the people she was serving. She wrote, "Today I learned a good lesson. The poverty of the poor must be so hard for them. While looking for a home I walked and walked till my arms and legs ached. I thought how much they must ache in body and soul, looking for a home, food and health. Then the comfort of Loreto came to tempt me. 'You have only to say the word and all that will be yours again,' the Tempter kept on saying . . . " But her extraordinary willpower and faith kept her going.

She was not alone for long. Soon volunteer helpers, mainly former students and fellow nuns, joined her in her work. But Mother Teresa realized that she would need more than temporary help to carry on. The Vatican gave her permission to start the Missionary Sisters of Charity, a new order of nuns who would dedicate themselves to caring for those abandoned by others. To the traditional nuns' vows of poverty, chastity, and obedience, Mother Teresa added a fourth: that they would devote themselves to "the poor and needy who, crushed by want and destitution, live in conditions unworthy of human dignity."

Within five years, the Sisters of Charity had grown to twenty-eight nuns. They lived without much more than the poor people they served. They each had few possessions: three saris, a cross, a rosary, a spoon, a plate, an umbrella, a water bottle, and a bucket for washing. They accepted no personal gifts and at social events would only accept a glass of water, which even the poorest of the poor could offer.

Their day began at 4:30 a.m. with prayers and mass, and by 8 a.m. the sisters were in the slums teaching children and caring for the sick. They returned to their convent for lunch and a short rest, and were back in the slum houses until dinner at 6 p.m. Dinner was followed by prayers, classes, and talks by Mother Teresa.

This lifestyle may sound harsh, but Mother Teresa found it liberating. She said, "The more you have, the more you are occupied, the less you give. But the less you have the more free you are. Poverty for us is a freedom. It is joyful freedom. There is no television here, no this, no that. But we are perfectly happy."

With the Sisters of Charity firmly established, Mother Teresa decided to move beyond education. She took on one of the hardest and most widely admired tasks: the care of the dying. In Calcutta, poor and homeless people are often left to die in the streets. Mother Teresa created Nirmal Hirday or the Home of the Pure Heart, a refuge for those nearing death. She took people off the streets, and gave them medical attention and a place to die with dignity. She said, "What is a beautiful death? A beautiful death is, for people who lived like animals, to die like angels—loved and wanted." Rituals were performed for the dying according to their religious beliefs: water from the Ganges River on the lips of Hindus, a reading from the *Quran* for Muslims, and Last Rites for Catholics.

The work of the Sisters of Charity continued to expand. In 1953, they moved into a simple three-story home in the center of Calcutta, which became known as the Mother House and was the base of Mother Teresa's mission. In 1955, Mother Teresa opened a second facility, the Nirmala Shishu Bhavan, or the Children's Home of the Immaculate Heart, for the increasing number of orphans and homeless youth in Calcutta. It was a two-story dwelling located a few blocks from the Mother House. There the sisters fed, clothed, and taught children. They also placed children for adoption and sent the older ones to regular schools or for training in a trade.

Like St. Francis, who also worked to help the poor, Mother Teresa soon found that she felt compelled to come to the aid of lepers who, for centuries, have been among the most despised and isolated people. Leper is the word used for a person with leprosy, or Hansen's disease, which is an infectious illness. Leprosy slowly destroys tissue, deforming fingers, toes, and facial bones. There is now a cure for lep-

The first step in becoming a saint in the Catholic Church is beatification. This requires proof of a miracle being performed by the candidate. In 2002, a woman said that when she placed a locket containing a picture of Mother Teresa on her abdomen, a beam of light emanated from the picture, curing her tumor. The Vatican recognized this as a miracle. Proof of a second miracle is required for Mother Teresa to be canonized (become a saint).

rosy, although the disease is still a problem in many countries.

In the 1950s there was a treatment for leprosy but no cure. Because people were so frightened of the illness, Mother Teresa was prohibited from tending to people suffering from leprosy at her home for the dying. She responded with a radical move: she started a mobile treatment clinic, which served lepers where they were living. Later she founded a village for lepers outside Calcutta. Shanti Nagar, or The Place of Peace, included thirty family homes, a hospital, a chapel, a convent, and a cottage industry school. People who staffed the village provided free medical treatment and also taught the residents trades such as weaving, carpentry, and shoe making. Eventually the Sisters of Charity established several leprosy outreach clinics throughout Calcutta, providing medication, bandages and food.

Leprosy, or Hansen's disease, is an infectious disease that has affected humanity since ancient times. Contrary to popular belief, leprosy does not cause body parts to simply fall off. The bacterium slowly destroys tissue, deforming finger, toes and facial bones. In the past, lepers were forced to live outside society and to carry bells warning others of their presence. Treatment for leprosy was introduced in the 1940s. Stronger therapy developed in the 1980s meant that people could be treated within their communities.

By the 1960s, Mother Teresa had opened hospices, orphanages, and leper houses all over India. Then she turned her attention to expanding the work of the Sisters of Charity throughout the world. Starting with Venezuela, the order opened houses in dozens of countries. They also began to respond to natural catastrophes such as famine, floods, and epidemics.

A memorial plaque dedicated to Mother Teresa in the Czech Republic

In 1969, a documentary was produced called *Something Beautiful for God,* which is about Mother Teresa and her order. A book with the same title followed. Mother Teresa's story caught the public's imagination and soon she was an international celebrity. The documentary's interviewer and writer, Malcolm Muggeridge, was awed by the power of Mother Teresa's presence. Muggeridge remembered seeing Mother Teresa off at the end of their time together. He said, "When the train began to move, and I walked away, I felt as though I were leaving behind me all the beauty and all the joy in the universe. Something of God's love has rubbed off on Mother Teresa."

Soon the woman who had been born as Agnes Gonxha Bojaxhiu was at ease with Popes and heads-of-state. She won many international honors, which she humbly regarded as "recognition that the poor are our brothers and sisters, that there are people in the world who need love, who need care, who have to be wanted." In 1979, Mother Teresa received the Nobel Peace Prize.

The Nobel was awarded "for work undertaken in the struggle to overcome poverty." John Sannes, chair of the Nobel Committee, said, "The hallmark of her work has been respect for the individual's worth and dignity. The loneliest and the most wretched, the dying destitute, the abandoned lepers have been received by her and her sisters with warm compassion devoid of condescension . . . "

In her Nobel speech, Mother Teresa spoke of her work. She said, "I am grateful to receive [the Nobel] in the name of the hungry, the naked, the homeless, of the crippled, of the blind, of the lepers, of all those people who feel un-wanted, unloved, uncared-for throughout society, people that have become a burden to the society and are shunned by everyone."

During the presentation, Mother Teresa was asked, "What

> "Everybody today seems to be in such a terrible rush, anxious for greater developments and greater riches and so on, so that children have very little time for their parents. Parents have very little time for each other, and in the home begins the disruption of peace of the world."
> —Mother Teresa

can we do to promote world peace?" She answered, "Go home and love your family." She spoke of this theme again in her Nobel Lecture, when she compared the poverty that leads to starvation to the kind of impoverishment she often encountered in affluent nations. She said, "I found the poverty of the West so much more difficult to remove. When I pick up a person from the street, hungry, I give him a plate of rice, a piece of bread, I have satisfied. I have removed that hunger. But a person that is shut out, that feels unwanted, unloved, terrified, the person that has been thrown out from society—that poverty is so hurtable [sic] and so much, and I find that very difficult."

Mother Teresa refused the conventional ceremonial banquet given to laureates, and asked that the $192,000 prize money be given to the poor people of India.

Not everyone regarded Mother Teresa's influence as entirely positive. She opposed abortion and used her Nobel speech as an opportunity to talk at length against it, calling it "the greatest destroyer of peace." She was criticized for this stance. She was also criticized for her unquestioning support for the hierarchy of the Catholic Church. While many sisters were pushing for change to include women in leadership roles in the church, Mother Teresa argued for the traditional role of submission for women.

Still, it would be hard to overestimate Mother Teresa's impact. She was small in stature—only 4 feet, 6 inches tall

(137 cm)—yet her influence was far-reaching. By 1996, she was operating missions in more than one hundred countries. Over the years, Mother Teresa's Sisters of Charity grew from twelve to thousands serving the "poorest of the poor" in four-hundred-and-fifty centers around the world.

Mother Teresa died on September 5, 1997, at the age of eighty-seven. Six years later, she was beatified—the first step in becoming a saint in the Catholic church—by Pope John Paul II and given the title "Blessed Teresa of Calcutta."

Witnessing the courage and determination that she demonstrated throughout her life, many people assumed that Mother Teresa was always sure of what she was doing. In reality, however, she struggled throughout her life with doubts. Her letters reveal how she wished for more direct guidance from God but often met only silence. To her spiritual advisor, Michael Van Der Peet, she wrote, "Jesus has a very special love for you. As for me, the silence and the emptiness is so great, that I look and do not see, listen and do not hear."

Mother Teresa often used the expression, "Give God permission to use you without consulting you." This seems to be how she viewed her life, driven to sacrifice without always being certain of her faith. She was "a pencil in God's hand," as she often referred to herself. Her ability to continue with such challenging work in the face of doubt demonstrates what her friend and legal advisor, Jim Towey said: "faith isn't about feeling, it's about will."

Alva Myrdal

Nobel Peace
Prize Laureate, 1982

Weaving the Strands of Love and Work

As an adult, Alva Myrdal led campaigns against poverty, racism, sexism—and, eventually, nuclear weapons. As a child, she knew what it was like to be poor and oppressed.

Alva Reimer was born on January 31, 1902, on a farm in rural Sweden. She was the eldest of five children. Alva learned important lessons about independence and resistance from her mother, Lowa—but she learned her lessons the hard way.

Lowa had rigid rules about Alva's appearance, about being obedient and polite, and about keeping the house germ-

> "A lot of emotional energy, that ought to be put at work and life itself, is now wasted away on reacting against the artificial limits put up around the female sex."
> —Alva Myrdal

free. Lowa had lost a brother and a sister to tuberculosis and lived in such fear of germs that she refused to kiss Alva or any of her other children. Worst of all for Alva—an avid reader—was that her mother banned books from the house because she regarded them as "dust traps." Alva rebelled by sneaking books in under her clothes.

Lowa was artistic and a great storyteller, but since she had few opportunities to express her talents in the family's small farming community, she directed all her energy to her children. Alva chafed under her mother's control and she and her sister would pray every night: "Dear God, please get Mom a job!" Because of her experience with her mother's frustrations, Alva advocated throughout her life for women to be able to work outside the home.

From her father, Albert, Alva learned how to turn frustration into positive action. Albert was a farmer who loved animals and the land on which he eked out a living. Albert hated inequality and was an active member of the social democratic "people's movement," which fought against economic injustice in Europe at the beginning of the twentieth century. Albert founded one of the first cooperative stores in Sweden, and young Alva used to hide under the table and listen during the co-op's board meetings. She regarded this secret eavesdropping as her first political education; from under the table, she learned the rules of order for running meetings. She also learned about campaign strategies and observed both women and men participating actively and equally.

One of Alva's first political struggles was her fight to get a good education. Alva was bright, loved primary school, and wanted more than anything else to continue on to high school. However, her parents thought further schooling would be a waste of money. They assumed that Alva would follow the traditional path for a girl and work at home until she got married.

Alva refused to accept this future for herself, and held onto her dream. She decided to earn the money to pay for her education. At fifteen, she began selling her embroidery and sewing. Later, she worked in a tax office. Alva divided her earnings into three equal portions: one for books, one for family, and one for her future education.

When she finally had the financial means, Alva proudly showed her parents the application to continue her studies in a nearby town. She would remember what happened next for the rest of her life. Her mother flew into a rage and tore the application to pieces. She ordered Alva to forget about such nonsense and warned her never to think about leaving the family again.

Alva was devastated, but she refused to give up. She talked to her father until he understood how important education was to her. He agreed to help, and requested that the local school board create a class for girls, separate from the boys. A class was started, but the girls didn't have a classroom of their own, which meant that they had to move continually from building to building—even though they paid more than ten times as much in fees as the boys did.

Alva later said that her struggles with her mother's oppressive rules and her family's lack of money gave her the ability "to identify with the downtrodden in general . . . It began with women first, [but soon] the identification became broader, more social, with the poor."

Alva used education to free herself, and that liberation

led to romance. When she was seventeen and attending the University of Stockholm, she met her future husband, Gunnar Myrdal, a brilliant law student who, according to their daughter, Sissela, not only loved her, but also "took her seriously in the way that mattered most to her: as a thinking person."

Alva and Gunnar's affection for one another was profound. As an adult, Sissela described her parents' marriage as, "a conversation which started when they first met and really went on as long as it could, despite the ups and downs. My mother always used to say that she had never met another man who was as interesting to talk to, and that she felt [this] to the end of her life." Their intellectual collaboration was a rich one; Alva called herself the "spray can of ideas," while Gunnar was the brilliant and methodical researcher.

Nonetheless, Gunnar made Alva's life difficult in many ways. He was a self-absorbed, temperamental man who was obsessed with his own work and constantly demanded Alva's attention. As far as Gunnar was concerned, his own career came first. He expected Alva to be responsible for maintaining their home and caring for their children. He also expected her to act as hostess for their large circle of visitors, which included many of the intellectual and artistic leaders of their time.

As a child, Alva had begged God to find her mother a job away from the house. Now, as an adult, she struggled to find a way to balance work and family. Alva was a pioneer when there were few role models available, and she was often criticized for the solutions she attempted. A cruel test of her ability to negotiate this new terrain came early.

In 1929, Alva and Gunnar both won Rockefeller Fellowships that would allow them to study in the United States. But their son, Jan, was only two years old, and accepting these important awards meant they would need to

leave him behind in Sweden. Although Alva's relatives encouraged her not to miss this opportunity and assured her
that Jan would be well taken care of on Gunnar's family
farm, Alva struggled with whether or not she should leave
her son. Gunnar insisted that she accompany him, however,
and she acquiesced.

She later wrote, "Did I therefore put marriage before par-
enthood? Yes, but not without gnawing guilt and an inner
sense of mutiny." Throughout her life she would refer to this
as the "first great mistake in her life," and the repercussions
from this leave-taking would come to weigh heavily upon
her.

Alva was both shocked and excited by what she discovered in the United States. She was shocked by the gap
between the rich and the poor, and by the racist treatment
of African Americans. But she was excited by the new field
of child psychology, which she studied at Yale University.
The idea of regarding a child as a unique individual in need
of a creative and affectionate environment appealed to Alva
immediately and affirmed her earlier rebellion against her
mother's severe, unaffectionate style of parenting. She returned to Sweden the following year, where she reunited with
Jan, and began her first social campaign.

Over the next two decades, Alva worked to create a new
"culture of parenting." She established preschools and a
teacher-training institute, and traveled the country lecturing on educational reform. She founded and joined women's
associations to fight for equal rights, and helped to end the
common business practice of firing women immediately when
they married or became pregnant.

Alva flourished intellectually as she found ways to address the treatment of women, children, and the poor. In
1934, she and Gunnar co-wrote *The Population Crisis*, a book
about poverty, housing, and education in Sweden. At first,

this book created a scandal for Alva. People were outraged that a woman had put her name on a book that included talk about sexuality and contraceptives. Ultimately, however, *The Population Crisis* was hugely influential in encouraging the development of national welfare programs in Scandinavia and elsewhere, and it made the Myrdal couple famous.

At the same time, mothering was requiring even more of Alva's attention. She now had two daughters, Sissela and Kaj.

Alva's quest to balance the demands of her work and her expanding family inspired her to design a house that could accommodate all of their needs. This radically modern home, Villa Myrdal, was built in Stockholm in 1937, and the family lived in it for more than a decade. The house included separate spaces for the children and the parents, easy-to-clean surfaces, curtain-free windows, and a movable partition to divide the master bedroom into separate spaces so that husband and wife could each have time alone.

After World War II, Alva continued to do important, high-profile work. Among other projects, she helped with plans to bring people from concentration camps to Scandinavia, she established a newspaper for refugees, and she advocated supporting refugees with jobs and education.

Although Alva had already accomplished a great deal, she later believed that her professional career did not really start until 1949, when she was forty-seven. On the day after her birthday, Alva sailed on her own for New York to become the first woman to work in a high-level position at the United Nations (UN). She became the Director of the Department of Social Affairs.

Alva had already turned down the same position earlier to accompany Gunnar when his job took him to Geneva. But now that her oldest child, Jan, had left home and her daughters could be cared for by a loving housekeeper, Alva

chose to put her own career first. She wrote to Gunnar, "For the *first time,* I shall hold up my work as against yours."

Alva thrived in New York and her diplomatic talents blossomed. Two years later, she moved to Paris to serve as Director of the Department of Social Sciences at UNESCO, an agency of the UN that was established after the war to

"It does not just happen. It is disclosed by science that practically one-half of trained intellectual resources are being mobilized for murderous purposes."
—Alva Myrdal

help with the reconstruction of Europe. Through her experiences in Paris and New York, Alva developed an international perspective on poverty and inequality, and she campaigned to bring her awareness and solutions to the world.

Her support of women and the poor did not go unnoticed. When Alva was appointed Sweden's ambassador to India in 1955, her reputation preceded her. She was met at the Delhi airport by a crowd of women and press photographers.

Alva toured India promoting Swedish democratic principles and pushing for access to education for Indian women, using the slogan: "An uneducated woman is a dangerous woman for society."

While in India, Alva became friends with Jawaharlal Nehru, the country's prime minister, and was inspired by his philosophy of peace. That philosophy was the basis of a campaign that occupied Alva for the final twenty years of her life.

When she returned to Sweden in 1961, Alva was asked to write a report on nuclear disarmament for the foreign minister. This request led to an intense period of study for her. The more she learned about the growing number of nuclear weapons in the world, the more committed she became to demanding that action be taken to disarm. Her research,

Alva said, "delivered the ammunition" for the "Unden Plan," which positioned Sweden and the other nuclear-free nations as leaders in the disarmament debate.

Alva's report was written at the height of the "Cold War" between the world's two superpowers—the United States and the Union of Soviet Socialist Republics (USSR). Both countries were stockpiling nuclear arms and people were terrified of nuclear annihilation. Many responded by building bomb shelters. Alva's response was to travel the country lecturing. She spoke dramatically on the link between poverty and disarmament: poor countries were spending money and using resources on bombs and armies rather than on social and economic development.

Alva made disarmament an important part of national politics in her own country. In 1966, at the age of sixty-five, she was elected to the Swedish Parliament. When she took office in 1967, she became the Cabinet Minister of Disarmament, the only such position in the world, and a post she held for twelve years.

From 1962 until 1973, Alva headed the Swedish delegation to the UN Disarmament commission. This is how one UN observer described her: "small and vivacious, her fair hair now gray, her blue eyes alight and her bright laughter always at the ready, she combined charm with determination, with an impressive mastery of scientific and technical detail." She became known as "the conscience of the disarmament movement" and was a tough opponent. One U.S. representative praised her debating skills, saying, "I bear many scars testifying to her effectiveness."

Alva was tireless. She fought for nuclear-free zones, a no-first-strike pledge from the nuclear powers, and a ban on nuclear testing. She promoted the 1967 Treaty of Tlatelolco, which created the first nuclear-free zone in the world and which all thirty-three Latin American countries signed.

Alva was nominated many times for the Nobel Peace Prize and was expected to win in 1981. When she didn't, there was an outcry in Norway, and $60,000 was raised and presented to her as the Norwegian People's Award. Alva was deeply touched. The next year, 1982, Alva finally won the Nobel Peace Prize.

But the suffering she experienced in her struggle to blend the demands of career and family had not ended. At the height of her public success—just before Alva was to receive the prize—she was deeply hurt by her son. The many accomplishments in Alva's life can be seen, at least in part, as a creative response to her mother's poor parenting. She must have felt wounded when her son, Jan,

Alva Myrdal's husband, Gunnar Myrdal, won the Nobel Prize for economics in 1974. Alva and Gunnar are the only couple in history to have each won Nobel Prizes independent of each other and in different categories. Three other couples (Marie Curie and Pierre Curie, Irene Joliot-Curie and Frédéric Joliot, Gerty Cori and Carl Cori) have shared Nobel Prizes in the same category.

by then an author, scholar, and filmmaker, published an autobiographical novel about his childhood. Jan portrayed his parents as cold, loveless over-achievers who treated their children "like small nasty cases" rather than children in need of affection. This was a sensational news event in Sweden.

The painful effect of Jan's criticism was softened somewhat by Alva's relationship with her daughters, in particular with Sissela. An established professor of ethics at Harvard, Sissela wrote a book about her mother in which she portrayed Alva in a much kinder light. According to Sissela, her mother was a woman who cared passionately about the fate of the world, yet also cared about the "women's realm"—food, clothing, and the home. Sissela saw her mother as struggling with the same concerns women face today: "how to make a life, how to weave the strands of love and work, how to achieve and maintain some balance and identity as an individual within a marriage, a family, and a community."

Alva was eighty-one years old and in poor health when she delivered her Nobel acceptance speech. Alva said it was a "trifle wearying" to have to keep repeating that continuing to build up the supply of nuclear weapons was irrational and unnecessary. However her persistence and commitment to peace overcame her weariness. She said, "I shall go on repeating, until the politicians get it into their heads, that when one has sufficient [arms], one does not need more."

When she died in 1986, the Swedish Prime Minister, Olof Palme delivered the eulogy at her funeral. He said: "Alva Myrdal had very clear eyes. They reflected the clarity of her thinking, the orderly and methodical way she handled every project, the happy faith in reason that carried her through life. In her eyes, you also encountered warmth, thoughtfulness, her ability to understand the situation of others . . . When you talk about Alva Myrdal, people become inspired."

Aung San Suu Kyi

Nobel Peace
Prize Laureate, 1991

"The Titanium Orchid"

On a hot, dry April day in 1989, in the lowlands along the Irrawaddy River, Aung San Suu Kyi—the new leader of Burma's pro-democracy movement—and her eight-car motorcade made their way to Danubyu, the next town on her campaign trail. All along the campaign route, thousands had come—at great risk—to hear her speak. The military junta had just passed a law that outlawed gatherings of more than five people. Anyone living along the route was forbidden to wave the peacock flag of the democracy movement or even to lean out their windows as Suu Kyi passed by their houses.

"Aung San Suu Kyi brings out something of the best in us. We feel we need precisely her sort of person in order to retain our faith in the future. That is what gives her such power as a symbol, and that is why any ill-treatment of her feels like a violation of what we have most at heart."
—Nobel Committee Chairman Francis Sejersted

They had been warned: If they disobeyed, they would be shot.

The smell of incense mixed with gasoline fumes hung in the midday air, occasionally pushed aside by a breeze scented with frying garlic and chilies from a nearby home. Suu Kyi and her supporters were accustomed to military harassment by the Tatmadaw, the Burmese army. Today, however, as they climbed out of the cars, they could feel that something was different. For one thing, there were many more soldiers and barricades set up than ever before, but stranger still was the quiet. The streets were deserted.

As Suu Kyi's group attempted to walk down the main street, soldiers began shouting abuse and pointed their rifles at her. The captain in charge yelled for her to turn around and leave. Suu Kyi ignored him and calmly continued to walk.

Three soldiers stepped forward to block her path, rifles pointed. "You really shouldn't bully me so much," Suu Kyi said with a smile, as she gently pushed down their weapons. "You must let us pass." The soldiers moved aside. Suu Kyi and her supporters moved ahead.

A group of six soldiers was waiting ahead, kneeling on the ground, guns pointing directly at Suu Kyi. The captain yelled, "If you do not go back . . . you will be shot." Suu Kyi kept walking.

"At the count of three . . . " the captain commanded.

Suu Kyi continued to walk forward, but alone now, presenting herself as an easy target so that only she would be killed.

"Two!"

At the last second, a major—seeing she was not going to stop—stepped in and called a halt to the countdown.

The Danubyu Incident, as it came to be known, was the moment when the Burmese people and the ruling military junta both realized the depth of Suu Kyi's courage and commitment to her country. Many spoke of her refusal to be intimidated even when confronted with death as proof that Suu Kyi was made of the same heroic cloth as her famous father, General Aung San. Her mother had been a diplomat and many also saw her mother's influence in Suu Kyi's elegant composure and in her perfect command of language. All were surprised, though, that this small, uncommonly beautiful woman, who had only recently returned to her country after a long absence, had taken to the role of political leader with such apparent ease. Suu Kyi and those closest to her were less surprised. They knew that she had been in training for just such a destiny all of her life.

Aung San Suu Kyi was born on June 19, 1945, in Rangoon, the capital city of Burma. She was named according to Burmese custom: "Aung San" from her father; "Suu" from her beloved grandmother; and "Kyi" from her strong mother. Together her name means "Bright Collection of Strange Victories."

Suu Kyi's father was a national hero. He had been a brilliant student, headed happily for life as a scholarly Buddhist monk when he became the leader of Burma's independence movement. He was soon famous for his integrity and his single-minded commitment to freeing Burma from British rule.

Aung San started the Burmese National Army and, as its leading general, he negotiated with the invading Japanese during World War II to help rid Burma of the British. When he realized that the Japanese had their own colonial plans for Burma, he managed to make a deal with the Allies—those countries that fought against the Nazis—to defeat the Japanese.

Aung San traveled to London, England in 1947 to negotiate independence from Britain and returned triumphantly to Burma. He immediately began planning for the peaceful transfer of power to a democratically elected Burmese government. Tragically, on July 19, 1947, just six months before independence was to be achieved, Aung San was assassinated by a rival general who was jealous of the Aung San's fame, and desired his power. The entire country mourned the death of Suu Kyi's father and the anniversary of his death became a national day of mourning.

Suu Kyi was only two years old when her father was killed, but his influence on her life was profound.

Suu Kyi's childhood home was open to constant visitors, including many important national and international figures, and often the army friends of her father. With admiration, they would tell the young girl tales of her father's adventures. These stories created an idealized figure for Suu Kyi. She learned from others that he was a man of great courage and trustworthiness who had changed the course of his life to help his country. As Suu Kyi said in a book she wrote about her father, "He was a man who put the interests of the country before his own needs." These same words describe the values that came to guide Suu Kyi's life: leadership as a duty often requiring great sacrifice in service to one's country.

As a child Suu Kyi had found her mother, Khin Kyi, "very strict at times," but she came to admire the values of self-discipline, honesty, and generosity that her mother instilled in her children. After her husband's assassination, Khin Kyi served as a member of parliament. She was known for her diplomatic skills of tactfulness, connecting quickly with others, and making decisions on the fly—all traits that were later admired in Suu Kyi.

Suu Kyi describes herself as having been a "normal naughty child" who wanted to be a soldier when she grew up. She recalls, "I wanted to be a general because I thought this was the best way to serve one's country, just like my father had done." However, at age ten, Suu Kyi discovered the magical world of books and her soldier ambitions were challenged by this new interest. She became, in her own words, "a bookworm." This was the dawning of an aspiration to become a writer.

Suu Kyi did well at her bilingual English and Burmese school. However, in 1960 her mother was appointed ambassador to India—she was the first woman in Burma to be appointed to such a high-ranking position—so fifteen-year-old Suu Kyi moved to Delhi, India. Suu Kyi finished high school there and, most importantly, discovered the writings of Mahatma Gandhi. Gandhi was the founder of the non-violent resistance movement that Suu Kyi would come to admire and follow. Suu Kyi also came to know and respect Prime Minister Jawaharlal Nehru. His principles of liberal democracy together with Gandhi's principles of non-violence were models that strongly influenced Suu Kyi's later work in Burma.

While Suu Kyi and her mother lived in India, however, Burma's democratic rule, for which Suu Kyi's father had fought so hard, was threatened and in 1962, the military, led by General U Ne Win, staged a *coup d'état* and took control of Burma. Over the next quarter century, Ne Win and his junta built up a brutal military regime that brought Burma to financial ruin and isolated the country from the rest of the world.

During this period, Suu Kyi left India to continue her

education in England at Oxford University. With her focus on being of help to her country in the future, Suu Kyi chose to study politics, philosophy, and economics rather than her first love, literature.

In contrast to the casualness of student dress in the 1960s, Suu Kyi stood out. Beautiful and "exotic," she was always impeccably dressed in her traditional Burmese silk *longyi* (sarong) and always wore a flower in her long black hair.

While at Oxford, Suu Kyi met her husband-to-be, Michael Aris. A handsome and brilliant scholar of Tibetan Studies, Michael was immediately smitten with Suu Kyi, but he was just about to leave for the Himalayan kingdom of Bhutan to be the personal tutor of the royal family. Suu Kyi felt that, because of Burma's colonial past, being seen to be dating a British man was not acceptable for any Burmese woman— particularly not for the "General's daughter." But Suu Kyi was falling in love.

When Michael moved to Bhutan, their courtship continued through letters. In one eight-month period, Suu Kyi wrote one hundred and eighty-seven letters, even though it took them weeks to reach the tiny, mountainous country where Michael was working. From the start of their relationship, Suu Kyi made it clear to her beloved that if her country needed her, she would have to return. She wrote, "I only ask one thing, that should my people need me, you would help me to do my duty by them." Michael agreed.

After finishing at Oxford, Suu Kyi moved to New York City to do post-graduate studies and was soon working for the United Nations (UN) on a financial committee that oversaw the approval of all UN budgets. The head of the UN at that time was U Thant, a charming Burmese man and an old friend of Suu Kyi's father. He was impressed with Suu Kyi and took a strong interest in her career.

Suu Kyi and Michael were married in 1972. She joined her husband in Bhutan, where she worked as an advisor to the King on UN affairs. The couple returned to England the next year for the birth of their son, Alexander. In 1977 their second son, Kim, was born.

> "It is not power that corrupts but fear. Fear of losing power corrupts those who wield it and fear of the scourge of power corrupts those who are subject to it."
> —Aung San Suu Kyi

Suu Kyi's life was full, but somehow she knew that she would be called on to return to Burma. That call came in March of 1988 when she received news that her mother had suffered a severe stroke. She flew alone to Rangoon the next day.

The months that Suu Kyi stayed to care for her mother coincided with a period of political unrest in Burma. Teashops are the center of Burmese social life and a confrontation in a tea shop in Rangoon—a fight between students and a relative of a military man over what music should be played—ended in five hundred riot police firing on an unarmed crowd. The next day thousands of students marched in protest, calling for democratic change in Burma. They were severely beaten by the military. In the marches that followed, many students were arrested and killed. Wounded protesters were brought to the Rangoon General Hospital where Suu Kyi was tending to her mother. The hospital became a hotbed of political discussion and planning. Suu Kyi listened carefully, yet remained focused on caring for Khin Kyi.

The protests grew. On July 23, General Ne Win resigned after twenty-six years of military dictatorship. There was great excitement as the chance for real change seemed possible and the news began to spread that "the General's daughter" had returned to Burma. On August 8, 1988, at a mass demonstration in Rangoon, hundreds of portraits of Suu Kyi's father were raised. But the army fired on the crowd of unarmed, peaceful protesters and three thousand people were killed.

Suu Kyi could no longer remain an observer as news of the horrific violence reached her. She recalled, "A life of politics held no attraction for me. But the people of my country were demanding democracy, and as my father's daughter, I felt I had a duty to get involved." She wrote an open letter to the government, which was now headed by Brigadier-General Sein Lwin, who was known as the Butcher of Rangoon for his leading role in the recent massacres of students and other protestors. In the letter, Suu Kyi demanded that the government prepare for democratic elections.

On August 26, half a million people came from all over Burma to hear Suu Kyi give her first public speech. As she stood in front of a huge photograph of her father, everyone remarked on how similar they were in looks, voice, and manner. Overnight, Suu Kyi became the symbol of hope and democracy for Burma. She was given the title of respect "Daw." Later, she was called Burma's "Titanium Orchid" because of her combination of strength and beauty.

The military reacted with extreme violence to the movement for democratic change and Suu Kyi's rising popularity, killing hundreds of protesters over the following months. The regime abolished all democratic institutions and banned all political gatherings. Many people were arrested and sentenced without trial. On September 18, the armed forces commanded by General Saw Maung seized control of Burma and announced the formation of the State Law and Order Restoration Council (SLORC). The only ray of light was the promise of a free election. Needing money, the military rulers had appealed to the international community for aid and promised to hold an election the next year.

Suu Kyi's house became the headquarters for the democracy movement and together with other prominent pro-democracy leaders she founded the National League for Democracy (NLD), a party dedicated to non-violent resistance.

Her mother died later that year, and Suu Kyi began to live the life of a highly disciplined general or politician. Her day began at four a.m. with strategy meetings with her staff. For months, she spent her afternoons in a tiny rented office where she held fifteen-minute meetings with all those wanting her counsel. The evenings she would spend alone reading and writing or with Michael and the boys, when their school and teaching schedules permitted and when the junta granted them visas.

In July 1989, after a speech in which Suu Kyi charged SLORC of lying to the people, trucks and soldiers blockaded her home. Suu Kyi was placed under house arrest. Surrounded by armed guards, Suu Kyi couldn't leave the house, and no one could visit her or her sons, who were already with her at the time of her arrest. Michael immediately flew to Burma and found Suu Kyi on the third day of a hunger strike. She was trying to protect students who had been taken from her house to an interrogation center. After twelve days, when good treatment for the students was assured, she ended the strike.

Despite her continuing detention and the arrest of other democratic leaders, Suu Kyi's NLD party won the September 1990 election by a landslide, securing eighty-two percent of the seats. Suu Kyi should have been the new prime minister of Burma, but the regime's leaders would not recognize the election results and refused to hand over power. Suu Kyi remained a prisoner in her own home.

The international community responded to Suu Kyi's courage and persistence by awarding her two major European

Anti-war protesters wearing Aung San Suu Kyi masks

human rights prizes that year, the Rafto Prize and the Sakharov Prize. The following year, 1991, she received the world's highest acknowledgment, the Nobel Peace Prize, for her non-violent struggle to restore democracy to Burma.

Suu Kyi's sons accepted the award on her behalf, standing in front of a large photograph of her. Suu Kyi used the $1.3 million prize money to establish a health and education trust for the Burmese people, which was run by Michael.

In April 1992, General Than Shwe became the leader of SLORC. Because of international pressure, he released Suu Kyi from house arrest in 1995. She had been captive in her house for six years. Upon release, she immediately spoke to the international press and resumed her campaign to bring democracy to Burma. She asked tourists not to visit Burma and foreign companies not to invest in her country until human-rights violations stopped. The junta reacted by threatening anyone who attended Suu Kyi's talks with twenty years in prison. The crowds of supporters grew bigger.

SLORC next sealed off her street during her talks. Suu Kyi resisted by walking to the barriers and greeting her supporters through barbed wire. The regime then sent groups of thugs—often as many as two hundred—to attack the crowds,

On June 18, 1989, the Burmese military junta passed a law that officially changed the English name of the country to Myanmar. In Burmese, both names are used, Myanma (Myanmar) is the more formal term, while Bamar (Burma) is used in everyday speech. But Myanmar is still not accepted as the official name by many people, including the pro-democracy movement, because the change was made by an illegitimate government and without consulting the citizens.

A "Free Aung San Suu Kyi Now"poster on the
European Parliament building in Brussels, Belgium.

 84

and thousands of her supporters were arrested. The harassment of Suu Kyi continued daily. In the summer of 1998, when she attempted to leave Rangoon to visit her supporters in other areas of the country, she was blocked by military police. She and her aides spent six days trapped in her car.

In January 1999, Suu Kyi faced one of the most difficult trials in her life. Michael was diagnosed with cancer in England and although he repeatedly requested permission to visit Suu Kyi one last time before he died, the military denied him an entry visa. They had not seen each other since 1995. The authorities suggested that Suu Kyi visit her husband in England instead. She faced an impossibly difficult decision. If she left Burma to be with Michael, she was sure she would never be allowed to return. If she stayed, she could continue to be a symbol of hope for her country and to help the families of those supporters who were in prison or had been killed. With Michael's support, she chose to remain in Burma, placing the needs of her country once more before her own.

Michael died on his 53rd birthday, March 27, 1999. British reporter, Maurice Chittenden, wrote the next day that Suu Kyi and Michael's relationship was "a love that tyranny could not crush."

In 2000, Suu Kyi was arrested again. Once again she had tried to leave Rangoon to visit supporters and was blocked in a mosquito infested swamp-land for nine days. Two hundred military police finally forced her back home. A month later, Suu Kyi tried to leave again. This time she was returned to house arrest for another two years.

In an interview, Suu Kyi spoke of the importance of her father as a guide during this difficult time: "When I was under house arrest, here on my own, I would come down at night and walk around and look up at his photograph and feel very close to him. I would say to him then: 'It's you and me, father, against them.'"

In May 2003, while touring through the Northern states of Burma, Suu Kyi's motorcade was attacked by a military-sponsored mob. Seventy of her supporters were murdered. Suu Kyi only survived because her quick-thinking driver fled the scene with her in the car. Nonetheless, she was arrested and kept in secret detention in Insein Prison for three months. She was then returned to house arrest where she remains to this day.

Suu Kyi has dealt with her confinement by following a routine of exercise, writing, playing the piano—until it recently broke—and reading well-worn detective novels. She also meditates and has often spoken about the importance of Buddhist meditation in her life. She says, "Meditation has helped to strengthen me spiritually in order to follow the right path."

Her health has suffered, however. In an interview she describes how "sometimes I didn't even have enough money to eat. I became so weak from malnourishment that my hair fell out, and I couldn't get out of bed. I was afraid that I had damaged my heart [and] then my eyes started to go bad." She paused for a moment, then pointed with a finger to her head and said, "But they never got me up here."

As a courageous symbol of non-violent defiance and courage, Suu Kyi continues to attract international support. Such widespread pressure, together with the courageous actions of the pro-democracy leaders and of the people of Burma may one day free Aung San Suu Kyi. Perhaps then, as the democratically elected leader of Burma, she will deliver her own Nobel acceptance speech to the world.

Rigoberta Menchú Tum

Nobel Peace
Prize Laureate, 1992

"My commitment to our struggle knows no boundaries."

Rigoberta Menchú Tum, a Maya woman from Guatemala, lived much of her young life in the midst of brutality and persecution. In 1980, when Rigoberta was twenty-one years old, her beloved father died a horrible death. He had been in the capital, Guatemala City, participating in a peaceful protest inside the Spanish embassy for better wages for farm workers. He and almost forty other *campesinos*—small-scale farmers and agricultural workers—were burned to death when the government-supported military stormed the embassy.

> "What I treasure most in life is being able to dream. During my most difficult moments and complex situations I have been able to dream of a more beautiful future."
> —Rigoberta Menchú Tum

A few months earlier, Rigoberta's younger brother Petrocinio had been tortured and murdered. And in another devastating incident, Rigoberta's mother died after having been kidnapped, raped, tortured, and mutilated by military forces. Distraught, yet inspired by her father's bravery and her mother's love, Rigoberta became an outspoken and fierce advocate for the rights of Indigenous people, not only in her homeland of Guatemala but also around the world. She said, "They've killed the people dearest to me . . . Therefore, my commitment to our struggle knows no boundaries nor limits."

Rigoberta's people, the Maya, are Native Americans from southern Mexico, Belize, Guatemala, Honduras, and El Salvador. The Maya include many different ethnic groups—each with its own traditions, language, and culture. An estimated six million Maya live in this area today. Some are integrated into their region's modern culture, while others live a more traditional life.

From 1960 to 1996, a brutal civil war ravaged much of Guatemala, a country in which the Maya represent close to half the total population. The others are mostly white (primarily Spanish descendents) and Ladino (mixed Indigenous and Spanish). The Maya were treated particularly cruelly by the military dictatorship. They were often caught in the middle of the violent conflict between the military and the opposing guerilla (armed, anti-government) forces. More than four hundred Indigenous villages were burned to the ground, and up to 200,000 Maya people were murdered by the military. These deaths account for more than eighty percent of the total lives lost during the war. Hundreds of thousands of children were orphaned, and more than a million people were forced to leave their homes for safer places, mostly in Mexico.

A *campesino* is a woman or man who lives in the country, usually a farmer or a person who works on the land. It comes from the Spanish word *campo*, which means the land or the countryside, and is related to the English word "peasant," which comes from *pais*—the French word for "country."

Rigoberta, a member of a large Maya group, the Quiché (also known as *K'iche'*), was born on January 9, 1959, into a family of farmers. Their farm was near the village of Laj Chimel, in a beautifully forested region in the mountains of northwestern Guatemala, the center of much of the violence. Rigoberta had five siblings, and they all worked on the family farm, where they grew traditional crops like corn and beans. Members of the family and their neighbors often traveled by truck to work on the enormous coffee and sugar plantations, or *fincas*. This was hot, backbreaking work, especially for the young children who picked coffee beans for fifteen hours a day, earning little more than pennies. But as hard as the plantation work was, it was safer than staying in the villages, which were often threatened by military invasions.

Rigoberta attended Catholic boarding schools and was a bright student who received scholarships in order to continue her studies. She became a catechist—a teacher of Catholic beliefs and principles—at the young age of eleven, and she also maintained a strong connection to the more land-based, traditional beliefs of the Maya people.

Rigoberta's father, Vicente, was active in an underground

union called the Committee of the Peasant Union (the *Comité de Unidad Campesina*, or CUC). The military was forcing Indigenous farmers to sell their land to the government for much less than it was worth. If the farmers refused, the military would destroy their homes, kill their farm animals, and often murder or injure the farmers and their families. The CUC, led by Vicente, encouraged the farmers to work together and to use non-violent means to resist the military forces.

Inspired by her father, Rigoberta became a union organizer and land rights activist. She traveled with Vicente to Indigenous communities where he spoke about land rights and fair treatment for workers. In her late teens and twenties, Rigoberta herself was active in the CUC, and it was through that experience, she says, that she "learned to fight, as a woman, for women's rights, and for fundamental human values."

Because of their involvement in these activities, both Rigoberta and her father were often at risk. Vicente had already been arrested and tortured, and Rigoberta had received threats, so they both lived away from their family, in hiding from the military. In fact, Rigoberta was hiding in a neighboring village when her mother was kidnapped, but she remembers vividly the last time she saw her mother alive. It was, she says, "my last chance to feel a mother's warmth . . . I shall never forget Mama fetching a little jar and taking out a red necklace, a medallion of the sun and five quetzales [Guatemalan currency]. She dropped it all in my hands, looked towards the rising sun and closed her eyes. She wept as she prayed. Then I left."

After the deaths of Rigoberta's mother, father, and brother, her two sisters joined the guerilla forces. Rigoberta, however, chose to work through peaceful channels. In 1981, she fled to Mexico, where she took sanctuary in the home of a Catholic bishop. Safely in exile, Rigoberta became an outspoken critic of the Guatemalan government and a powerful voice for Indigenous peoples' rights. With other Guatemalan exiles, she co-founded the United Representation of the Guatemalan Opposition (*Representación Unitaria de la Oposición Guatemalteca*, or RUOG).

Shortly after, Rigoberta gained a new level of international attention for her cause. In Mexico, she had been both fascinated and dismayed to learn how the oppression of the Maya people in Guatemala was repeated in Indigenous communities throughout North and South America and across the globe. She and other members of RUOG had formed an alliance with the International Indian Treaty Council, an organization working on behalf of Indigenous groups across South and North America, and were invited by the Council to address the United Nations in Geneva. She continued to lobby the UN for many years.

Rigoberta's work at the UN was never easy. Members of RUOG were not permitted to address the UN committees directly. Instead, they had to fight for opportunities to speak and to find an audience who would listen. The Guatemalan government lobbied hard to keep Rigoberta's stories from being heard. But she was determined, and the members of RUOG worked hard to call the attention of the international community to the serious human-rights violations in Guatemala. Rigoberta describes her experience at the UN: "The police would come and tell me, 'Madam, this is a government area, you can't come in.' I would pretend that I didn't understand English, but they would throw me out anyway. Then I would go back in again. For twelve years I steam-rolled . . . down the UN corridors, battering down all its doors."

Eventually, her perseverance paid off. In 1986, the UN passed a resolution that recognized the human rights abuses that were happening in Guatemala. While Rigoberta and her *compañeros*—her companions in the struggle—knew that this would not guarantee peace in their country, it was an important step toward recognition of the Indigenous people's struggle, and they hoped that it might help to avoid further deaths. It was also the first step toward the historic Peace Accord, a treaty between the Guatemalan government and the guerillas, which was signed a decade later in 1996.

Rigoberta's work at the UN was part of a larger struggle to have the rights of Indigenous peoples around the world recognized and respected. She became a key player in the Working Group on Indigenous Populations, whose aim was to develop and ratify a Universal Declaration of the Rights of Indigenous Peoples. This important document took twenty years to develop—143 countries finally voted to adopt it in 2007—and it is meant to ensure that all countries recognize and respect their Indigenous populations.

The Maya have an impressive artistic and intellectual history that lives on in art and weaving and can still be glimpsed in architectural remains. Rigoberta is proud of her heritage—she often wears the traditional *huipil* and *corte*, or blouse and skirt, of her home community—but she is frustrated that traditional tourist images are all that some people know of her country. "The other face of Guatemala is the face of repression, of the war, of many dead," she says. And she insists on recognition of the dignity of modern Maya: "We are not myths of the past, ruins in the jungle or zoos. We are people and we want to be respected, not to be victims of intolerance and racism."

In 1983, as part of her struggle to have Indigenous experiences more widely recognized, Rigoberta embarked on a project that would have enormous consequences—both good and bad. She published the story of her life, *I, Rigoberta Menchú: An Indian Woman in Guatemala*. Elisabeth Burgos-Debray, a Spanish-speaking anthropologist from Paris, made eighteen audiotapes of conversations she had had with Rigoberta. Elisabeth then edited, revised, and arranged the stories. The book, which exposed the brutality of Guatemala's civil war, has been translated into twelve languages and is taught in high schools and universities around the world.

The story begins: "My name is Rigoberta Menchú. I am twenty-three years old." She explains, "This is my testimony . . . I'd like to stress that it's not only my life, it's also the testimony of my people. It's hard for me to remember everything that's happened to me in my life since there have been many very bad times, but, yes, moments of joy as well. The important thing is that what has happened to me has happened to many other people too: My story is the story of all poor Guatemalans. My personal experience is the reality of a whole people."

Political leaders in Guatemala responded in anger. They accused Rigoberta of being a guerrilla, called her a communist, and threatened her life. The book was banned in Guatemala during the 1980s, even though people around the world were reading it and learning the story of the Maya people.

In the book *I, Rigoberta Menchú* Rigoberta says, "Life has been our teacher. The horrors I have suffered are enough

> ". . . instead of giving a rifle to somebody, build a school; instead of giving a rifle, build a community with adequate services. Instead of giving a rifle, develop an educational system that is not about conflict and violence, but one that promotes respect for values, for life, and respect for one's elders. This requires a huge investment. Yet if we can invest in a different vision of peaceful coexistence, I think we can change the world, because every problem has a nonviolent answer."
>
> —Rigoberta Menchú Tum

for me. And I've also felt in the deepest part of me what discrimination is, what exploitation is. It is the story of my life. When you understand this, when you see your own reality, a hatred grows inside you for those oppressors that make the people suffer so." But despite this hatred, Rigoberta always sought peaceful means to confront the war and the military. A Guatemalan journalist wrote that Rigoberta "makes those who are guided by hate, racism, selfishness, and stupidity tremble."

In 1987, Rigoberta shook up the military leaders and politicians in Guatemala once again when she narrated a documentary film, *When the Mountains Tremble,* a brutal and graphic depiction of the sufferings of the Maya people. The next year, when Rigoberta attempted to return to Guatemala, she and other UN representatives were arrested and accused by the government of being "subversives, communists, feminists, or *indiginistas* . . . rebels who, by some mistake, were still alive." Rigoberta was singled out with formal charges of "public disorder, organizing peasants to rebel against the government, and being a national security risk." Demands from other countries eventually ensured that she and the others were safely released.

In 1992, Rigoberta was awarded the Nobel Peace Prize, in honor of the commitment and sacrifices she had made in her struggle for the rights of Indigenous people around the world. At thirty-three, she was the youngest person and the first Indigenous person ever to receive the prize. In their press release, the Nobel committee called her a "vivid symbol of peace" and said that the prize is "in recognition of her work for social justice and ethno-cultural reconciliation based on respect for the rights of Indigenous peoples."

Rigoberta humbly acknowledged that the Peace Prize belongs to all those who are engaged in the same struggle. In her acceptance speech, she said, "I consider this Prize, not as a reward to me personally, but rather as one of the greatest conquests in the struggle for peace, for human rights, and for the rights of the Indigenous people, who, for five hundred years, have been split, fragmented, as well as the victims of genocides, repression, and discrimination."

Church bells rang out in Guatemala and people celebrated in the streets when it was announced that Rigoberta had won the Nobel Peace Prize. Shouts of "Viva, Rigoberta!" filled the air. The chief military leader, however, said that she should not have received the award because she "defamed the fatherland" and "endangered Guatemala." She received death threats and deliveries of funeral flowers, and was forced to hire bodyguards. Still, most Guatemalans, as well as her supporters around the world, rejoiced.

With her Peace Prize money, Rigoberta established the Rigoberta Menchú Tum Foundation. Her goal, she said, was to use the money "as an exhortation to everyone to work for a lasting peace," and to honor her father's memory and the Indigenous struggle for their land. The Foundation's inspiring Code of Ethics states: "There is no peace without justice; no justice without equality; no equality without development; no development without democracy; no democracy without respect to the identity and dignity of cultures and peoples."

In 1994, Rigoberta returned to Guatemala. She decided that she could do more good from within her home country. She worked toward a peaceful end to the war, and, in anticipation of the 1995 federal election, her foundation launched a National Campaign for Civic Participation, which encouraged women and Indigenous people to vote. Rigoberta was also the official spokesperson for the UN International Decade of Indigenous Peoples (1994 to 2003), a campaign that increased awareness of Indigenous peoples' issues across the globe, and also provided opportunities for discussions and celebrations of Indigenous cultures.

Rigoberta attending PeaceJam in 2006

In 1996, Guatemala's right-wing military government and left-wing guerrilla forces signed the Peace Accord, an historic document designed to find a peaceful end to the war. The fighting stopped, although Maya people were still discriminated against and disadvantaged. There were few Mayas in leadership roles in government, and—in a country where many live in poverty—the Maya communities were, and still are, the poorest.

The road to peace would be challenging. In 2004, Guatemala's President Oscar Berger appointed Rigoberta Menchú Tum as "goodwill ambassador" with the responsibility of monitoring the agreements in the Peace Accord. While she had previously been an enemy of the ruling government, Rigoberta was now cautiously attempting to work within the system. Her approach, as always, was balanced and straightforward. She said, "I believe that in Guatemala the solution is not confrontation between Indigenous and Ladinos. Rather, we need a country where we can live together with mutual respect."

However, the accounts of Rigoberta's experiences would not go unchallenged. In 1999, an American academic published a book claiming that many of the events outlined in *I, Rigoberta Menchú* had been made up and were not Rigoberta's or her family's own experiences. Rigoberta was placed in the awkward position of having to defend her life story. She acknowledged that some of the incidents in the book are not purely autobiographical, and she reminded critics that she had been honest about this from the first lines of the book, in which she states that these are stories of "all poor Guatemalans." She ended the discussion with the words, "If you want to debate, I ask you to go to the mass graves, go to the area where there are the remains of our dead. I ask for respect for my father who was buried alive and my brother who was tortured."

There were calls to have her Peace Prize taken back, but the Nobel committee members were unwavering in their support of Rigoberta. They said the Prize was awarded in recognition of her lifetime of work on behalf of Indigenous people and for human rights, not merely for her personal story and her own suffering.

In the federal elections in September 2007, Rigoberta ran for President of Guatemala—the first Maya to do so. "Guatemala has been ready to have a Mayan president for more than two hundred years," she stated, as she courageously faced a racist and sexist opposition. One opposing politician told her to "go and sell tomatoes at the market, Indian." But Rigoberta didn't back down. She did not win the election, but her courage and commitment ensured that Indigenous people's rights were prominent in the election process.

Rigoberta continues to shine as a bright symbol of peace, in her own country and across the globe. In his Nobel presentation speech, Francis Sejersted, Chairman of the Norwegian Nobel Committee, said, "By maintaining a disarming humanity in a brutal world, Rigoberta Menchú Tum appeals to the best in all of us, wherever we live and whatever our background. She stands as a uniquely potent symbol of a just struggle."

Jody Williams

Nobel Peace
Prize Laureate, 1997

"Go Forth As Troublemakers"

Have you ever had an experience with a bully? Jody Williams has. Her older brother was born deaf and later developed schizophrenia, a mental illness. As a child, he was often teased by bullies, but Jody defended him and became his protector. She said, "I couldn't understand why people would be mean to him because he was deaf. That translated into wanting to stop bullies being mean to people just because they are weak." All of her life, Jody has stood up to bullies, whether they were mean kids or irresponsible governments. Her desire to defend the vulnerable led her to

99

> "Please, use your individual power. Use that power for change. Seize that power and go forth as troublemakers for positive change on our very small planet."
> —Jody Williams

what would become her life's work.

Jody didn't always know what she wanted to do with her life. She was born in 1950 in Brattleboro, a peaceful town in rural Vermont and went off to university without having a clear idea of the shape she wanted her future to take. She had some strong ideas about the things she didn't want, though. She remembers thinking, "I didn't want to grow up, have 2.2 kids, get married, the whole white picket fence thing."

Jody decided to study languages, and in 1972 received her Bachelor of Arts degree with a specialization in teaching English as a Second Language (ESL). She continued her education and was awarded her Master's degree in teaching Spanish and ESL, and a second Master's degree in International Relations.

Like many young people unsure of their destinies, Jody decided to travel and see more of the world. She taught ESL in Mexico and the United Kingdom, and then returned to the United States, where she taught in Washington, DC. But she wasn't inspired by her work, and began looking for something more challenging.

Politics called. In the 1970s the United States was involved in the controversial war in Vietnam. Jody was offended by her country's behavior—seen by many as bullying—and she joined in protests with other young people in the U.S. and around the world. Jody says, "I was concerned about what was happening in Vietnam, so I began to learn that I could ask questions about foreign policy and try to take action to make a difference."

Her life took on a new focus. She began attending political meetings where she learned about U.S. military intervention in El Salvador and other countries in Central America. She worked for aid organizations in Central America, was a co-ordinator of the Nicaragua-Honduras Education Project, and then became deputy director of Medical Aid for El Salvador, a Los Angeles-based charity.

The wars in Central America were brutal, and Jody witnessed firsthand the horrible deaths and injuries caused by landmines. When she saw the children who had lost arms and legs in explosions, her life's work became clear. She says, "I didn't pick landmines, the issue picked me. I saw the devastating and crippling effects of landmines, especially on women and children. A country littered with thousands of landmines does not have peace." Jody's mission would be to help rid the world of these cruel devices.

Still, she had to wait for an opportunity to begin that work in earnest. Finally, after ten years of working in Central America, Jody was approached by two organiza-tions—the Vietnam Veterans of America Foundation and Medico International (a German group)—about starting an international anti-landmine campaign. At that time, a few organizations were helping victims of landmines, and oth-ers were concentrating their efforts on de-mining—removing landmines from abandoned war zones. Jody and others recognized the value of coordinating the efforts of the anti-landmine groups. Four more international organizations stepped up, and in 1992, Jody became the founding coor-dinator of the International Campaign to Ban Landmines (ICBL).

Her foe was formidable. Jody calls landmines "the per-fect soldier." They don't need food or water. They don't need instructions or even uniforms. Anti-personnel landmines are designed to explode when a person walks over them or picks them up, and they are a frighteningly effective weapon for killing people. The problem is they don't know who they're killing, or when. Sometimes for years after a war has ended, landmines continue to murder and injure. No one is safe: landmines injure and kill women walking to get water, farmers working in their fields, and children playing. The mines themselves are often brightly colored, attracting the attention of curious children.

The problem the ICBL faced was huge. In the late 1980s and early 1990s, millions of landmines littered dozens of countries. People trying to help—refugee and development organizations, humanitarian and medical relief groups—could not safely or effectively do the work they were meant to. As well, thousands of people were being killed or seriously injured on a daily basis.

Jody Williams giving a speech for the
Japanese Campaign to Ban Landmines.

De-mining is dangerous and terrifying work. It has to be done mine by mine, each courageous worker prodding the ground with a stick. When workers find a mine, they dig a hole around it and either blow it up in a controlled way or remove it to a remote site where many landmines are blown up at once.

But de-mining efforts and aid to landmine victims were not enough. Jody understood that the ICBL needed to stop the production and sale of landmines *before* they were placed in the ground and had the opportunity to hurt people. The only solution would be to secure a complete international ban on landmines. No small task!

Jody was a no-nonsense and determined worker. Over the next five years, she coordinated the building of a coalition of more than thirteen hundred governmental and non-governmental organizations in more than eighty-five countries. As exciting as this was, this group estimated that it would take them thirty years to achieve their goal of a complete international ban on anti-personnel landmines.

Still, they pressed on because the need was so great. In Cambodia, the worst affected nation, between four and

In a heavily mined area of Croatia, the anti-mine campaign asked locals who had information about where mines were buried to come forward. They didn't get a response. A few weeks later a young man walked through the woods, collecting firewood. He stepped on a mine and lost both his legs in the explosion. Shortly after, an older man arrived at the campaign office and revealed that he had been responsible for the mines in that section of the woods, and that the young man who had been so badly injured was his son. He offered his help, and the remaining mines were cleared from the area.

Before her tragic death, the late Diana, Princess of Wales, became an outspoken advocate for the anti-landmine campaign. She traveled to Angola and Bosnia, two of the world's worst-affected countries, where she met with victims of landmines and government officials. Her efforts received extensive media attention, and Princess Diana was able to give a human face to landmine victims. Her high profile and popularity raised international awareness of the campaign and gave an enormous boost to the ICBL.

six million landmines covered more than fifty percent of the country. Afghanistan had more than nine million land-mines, and Yugoslavia had six million. There were nine million in Angola, a million in Mozambique, and an-other million in Somalia. In all, an estimated two hundred million mines lay waiting to murder and maim in countries around the world.

Jody organized a series of international landmine conferences where delegates could talk about how they would achieve their objectives, which included increasing medical and financial aid for landmine victims. At each conference, the ICBL grew stronger and moved closer to the process of negotiating an international landmine treaty. Some governments were interested but skeptical, while others were downright resistant.

Jody's determination grew stronger, and she embraced her role as a "troublemaker." "Life isn't a popularity contest," she says. "I really don't care what people say about me—and believe me, they've said plenty. For me, it's about trying to do the right thing, even when nobody else is looking. The only thing that changes this world is taking action." And Jody just wouldn't give up. She explains, "You have to be willing to keep pushing when governments see you coming and want to run, when you know they want you to 'shut up'!" Jody's courage was a major force behind the coalition. Susannah Sirkin, the Deputy Director of Physicians for Human Rights, said that Jody "has never been reluctant to stand in front of a general or world leader with a conviction that she was right on this issue, and tell them what needs to be done."

In October 1996, the ICBL hosted a meeting in Ottawa, Canada. Countries that had expressed an interest in the ban were invited to develop a declaration of intent, which the ICBL hoped would lead to a final treaty. This meeting—called the Ottawa Process—ended with an unexpected but welcome turn of events. Lloyd Axworthy, Canada's Minister of Foreign Affairs, shocked everyone present by challenging each country to return to Ottawa in one year to sign an international treaty banning anti-personnel landmines.

According to the International Campaign to Ban Landmines (ICBL), an estimated 15,000 to 20,000 people are killed or injured by landmines each year. This means 1,500 new casualties each month, more than 40 a day, at least two per hour. Most of these casualties are civilians living in countries that are at peace.

This surprise move by the Canadian government, now known as the "Axworthy Challenge," provided exactly the momentum that the ICBL needed. One year later, in September 1997, eighty-nine countries met in Oslo, Norway to complete the negotiations, and in December 1997, one hundred and twenty-two countries met in Ottawa to sign the landmark treaty, which is formally called "The Convention on the Prohibition of the Use, Stockpiling, Production and Transfer of Anti-Personnel Mines and on their Destruction." The treaty also guaranteed that countries would increase their spend-

Jody Williams at the Nobel Women's Initiative's
first international conference in Galway, Ireland.

ing on de-mining efforts and victim assistance. This was an enormous accomplishment in a very short period of time. Instead of the thirty years they had anticipated, the ICBL moved from vision to signed treaty in a mere six years!

On the morning of October 10th, 2007, Jody was at her quiet home in Putney, Vermont, after celebrating her forty-seventh birthday with her family. She looked outside and saw dozens of cars and reporters. She walked out in her jeans and bare feet, and received the surprise news that she and the ICBL were going to share the Nobel Peace Prize for 1997.

True to her style, Jody took advantage of the media coverage to criticize American President Bill Clinton, who had refused to sign the treaty (as of 2008, the U.S. is one of thirty-seven countries, including Iran, Burma, China, and North Korea, who have still not signed). She didn't receive the traditional congratulatory phone call from the then-President, and she said, "I think if the President can call the winner of the Super Bowl, he should call the Nobel Peace Prize winner. It's tragic that President Clinton does not want to be on the side of humanity."

In presenting the Peace Prize to an individual as well as to the ICBL, the Nobel committee not only recognized Jody's work, but also the efforts of thousands of ordinary people around the world. Jody said, "[the Nobel Committee] wanted to highlight the key role that individual citizens can play in solving the critical issues that face the world today."

Jody's work didn't end with the signing of the treaty. She travels the world as a campaign ambassador for ICBL, promoting their ongoing projects and missions. The ICBL fundraises to support de-mining operations and to provide aid for landmine victims, and continues to raise awareness of landmine issues. The ICBL also has a Youth Ambassador and a Youth Against War program, working with young people

Jody and her dog, Stella

in schools internationally to bring awareness to the ongoing landmine crisis.

More than ten years after receiving the Nobel Peace Prize, Jody continues to challenge and inspire activists around the world. Speaking to teens, Jody said, "Don't come and tell me that you are really worried about global warming, gender equality, the rights of gays, because I am going to ask you what you're doing about those issues . . . Peace is not a rainbow, it is not [about singing songs] and [reciting] poetry. That is not peace. When you talk about a different world, a different kind of global security, you're talking about hard work. It's hard work."

At a recent lecture at the University of Alberta in Edmonton, Canada, Jody declared, "There's nothing magic about it at all. It's getting up off your butt and taking action to do something about the things you complain about . . . Look at me. I volunteered, I got a cheesy little job, I got another little job and then I got the Nobel Prize. See? Easy."

Shirin Ebadi

Nobel Peace
Prize Laureate, 2003

Fierce Defender of the Silent

Imagine. One day you are a respected judge, working with others to bring about positive change in your country. You work hard to help your political friends come to power and when they succeed, you celebrate together. The next day, these same friends tell you that, because you are a woman, you can no longer sit as a judge. Then they demote you to secretary in the same law courts you ran, and they forbid you to practice law. How would you respond to this betrayal? Would you stay in your country or leave for a more welcoming place? This is the real nightmare that Iranian human rights

> "My aim is to show that those governments that violate the rights of people by invoking the name of Islam have been misusing Islam."
> —Shirin Ebadi

lawyer Shirin Ebadi woke up to in 1978.

Shirin—the name means "sweet" in Persian—Ebadi was born in Hamedan in northwestern Iran in 1947. She spent her childhood in the city of Tehran, in a family home filled with kindness. Shirin recalls her childhood home with affection. "The house was quite large, two stories tall and full of rooms, a veritable playground for my siblings and me . . . There was a pool in the middle where a few silvery fish swam, and on summer evenings our beds were carried outside, so that we could fall asleep under the stars."

Shirin remembers that her first stirrings of her lifelong commitment to fairness and human rights started when she was only a child. She recalls, "I always had a feeling during childhood, almost like a calling, which I could not name then, but I later found that it was about seeking justice, a certain commitment to justice. When I was a child, whenever I would see children fighting, I would naturally try to defend the underdog, the weakest. I even got beaten up myself a couple of times doing that!"

Shirin's own mother, Minu Yamini, might have welcomed such a fierce defender. In her youth, Minu had dreamt of being a doctor. However, her conservative family would not permit it because they felt that this was an inappropriate job for a woman, and she never fully recovered from the disappointment. Minu was devoted to her children, but suffered from severe anxiety and was often ill. Shirin says, "I can't recall a single day when my mother seemed truly happy."

In many cultures, restrictive interpretations of religious books have contributed to the repression of women and girls.

Fortunately for Shirin, her father did not agree with such ideas. At the time of Shirin's birth, her father, Mohammad Ali Ebadi, was the city's chief notary public and a professor of law. He was also an exceptional parent and husband. Shirin says, "Circumstance and era conspired to keep my mother from a university education, but at least she ended up marrying a man as unpatriarchal as could be imagined, for his time." A patriarchy is a kind of society in which men hold power and women are largely excluded from it. In a patriarchy, men and boys get better educations and better jobs than women and girls do. They also enjoy more social freedom.

But Shirin's father believed that girls deserved the same opportunities as boys, and Shirin took his "radical" view for granted. She says, "It didn't strike me as exceptional that my parents did not treat my brother differently from their daughters. It seemed perfectly natural, and I assumed everyone else's families were the same way."

When Shirin was older she realized how unique her father was. "I saw how my upbringing spared me from the low self-esteem and learned dependence that I observed in women reared in more traditional homes. My father's championing of my independence, from the play yard to my later decision to become a judge, instilled a confidence in me that I never felt consciously, but later came to regard as my most valued inheritance."

Shirin's father wanted independence, not just for his daughter, but also for his homeland. Iran is rich in oil. At the time of Shirin's birth, Iran was ruled by Shah Mohammed Reza Pahlavi. He had been helped to power by Western countries, including the United States and Britain, and in exchange had given those countries easy access to Iran's oil.

Shirin's father supported a politician named Mohammad Mossadegh, who was elected prime minister in 1951. Mossadegh became very popular when his parliament voted to put Iran's British-owned oil industry back under Iranian control. But there were those, both within Iran and countries elsewhere, who were afraid they would lose access to the oil. Eventually, these forces organized the overthrow of Mossadegh's government in 1953. He was imprisoned and the Shah was reinstated as the country's leader.

One of Shirin's strongest memories is of the day Mohammed Mossadegh was overthrown. Because her father had supported Mossadegh, he lost his job after the prime minister's government was ousted. Shirin remembers that her father paced around the house, but she didn't know why. His career was set back and from then on he forbade discussions of politics in the house.

Shirin did well in school and started to study law at the University of Tehran in 1965. Under the re-instated Shah, the influence of Western society was all around—European films, miniskirts and beehive hairdos—but this influence did not extend to the conservative social lives of Shirin and her friends. Instead of dating, they always socialized in groups, and their classes were divided, with women in the front and men in the back.

The university was the center of political debates and student protests. Many Iranians resented the Shah's close ties to the United States. They felt that his government was corrupt and extravagant, and that his security forces were too brutal. Some also believed that traditional Iranian values, especially Islamic ones, were being lost. But Shirin was drawn to these protests as much for the chance to socialize as for the political content. She remembers, "I scarcely suspected that such protests would . . . one day alter the course of our lives, send shock waves around the world, and produce the twentieth century's last great revolution."

Shirin received her law degree, finishing at the top of her class. In 1969, she became the first woman in Iranian

history to serve as a judge, and in that same year was the first Iranian woman to achieve Chief Justice status. She continued her education and received a Master's degree with honors in private law in 1971.

Shirin enjoyed her new career even though it complicated her prospects of marriage. When men found out she was a judge, they quickly lost interest in her. Shirin attributed this attitude to "educated, supposedly modern Iranian men as well as traditional ones [who] simply preferred to be superior and more important than the women they married."

"How can you defy fear? Fear is a human instinct, just like hunger. Whether you like it or not, you become hungry. Similarly with fear. But I have learned to train myself to live with this fear."

—Shirin Ebadi

However, in 1975 a young electrical engineer named Javad Tavassolian proposed to Shirin. She responded with a unique proposal of her own. She suggested a test to find out if they were right for each other. They would spend the next six months getting to know each other, and then spend a month apart. Javad agreed and they did just that. Their devotion passed the test and they were married soon after. Shirin said, "[my husband] was the second central man in my life who tried to strengthen, rather than inhibit, my independence."

Javad was supportive of Shirin's work but traditional in his views of household duties. Despite her busy schedule as a judge, Shirin was responsible for all the shopping, cooking, and cleaning in the household. She views this as a necessary concession: "That Javad championed my career was itself tremendous; if the balance of household work swung entirely in my direction, that was a compromise I was willing to make."

Meanwhile, many Iranians were increasingly unhappy with the Shah's rule. In 1978, anti-Shah protesters began calling for a revolution that would replace what they felt was a corrupt monarchy with a government run on strict religious principles. Ayatollah Khomeini, a conservative Iranian cleric who had been in exile in Iraq because of his fiery sermons attacking the Shah, called for Iranians to expel government ministers from their offices. Wanting to take part, Shirin joined in on the storming of the office of the Minister of Justice. However, instead of the Minister, the protestors found an elderly judge.

"You!" he cried, when he saw Shirin. "You of all people, why are you here? Don't you know that you're supporting people who will take your job away if they come to power?" Shirin remembers her reply as "self-righteous to the core." She said, "I'd rather be a free Iranian than an enslaved attorney." This same judge would later remind Shirin of her words whenever they met.

Shirin continued to support the opposition to the ruling monarchy and her endorsement encouraged the support of other Iranian women. Shirin felt she had more in common with the various factions of the opposition than she did with the increasingly brutal rule of the Shah. On January 16, 1979, amidst massive protest, the Shah fled Iran, ending two thousand years of rule by Persian kings.

When the Ayatollah assumed control of the Iranian government a month later, Shirin joined the celebrations. Before long, though, she saw things differently. "That day, a feeling of pride washed over me that in hindsight makes me laugh . . . It took scarcely a month for me to realize that, in fact, I had willingly and enthusiastically participated in my own demise. I was a woman, and this revolution's victory demanded my defeat."

Ayatollah Khomeini immediately introduced new laws

that relied on very conservative interpretations of Islam. Among other things, the place of women in Iranian society was to be radically altered. Shirin and other female judges were demoted because they were women. The new religious rulers considered women to be too emotional and believed they lacked reason. "Islam," Shirin explains, "like any religion, is subject to interpretation. It can be interpreted to oppress women or interpreted to liberate them." Shirin was forced to work as a secretary in the very courtroom over which she had presided as a judge.

In 1980, the country's new Islamic penal code, *Sharia Law*, was adopted overnight. Reading the morning paper, Shirin learned about the new legal status of Iranian women. She was filled with rage. "The grim statutes that I would spend the rest of my life fighting stared back at me from the page," she recalls. "[T]he value of a woman's life was half that of a man," explains Shirin. For example, under these new laws, if a car hit both a man and a woman on the street, the woman's family would receive half as much money as the man's family. Or if a woman wanted to travel she needed her husband's written permission.

The new laws gave the *komiteh*—the morality police— wide-ranging power to patrol public spaces looking for women who weren't dressed according to Islamic law. All women were required, in public, to wear loose clothing that covered their entire body, including their arms and legs, and also a *hijab*—head scarf—to cover their hair. These patrols could appear at any moment, which made being in public a frightening experience for women. Shirin herself was arrested by the *komiteh* on two occasions. She believes that the real aim of this harassment was to create "a climate of fear . . . a fear so pervasive that it would keep women at home, the place where traditional Iranian men believed they should be."

Shirin could not tolerate what she saw as injustice in

this new treatment of women. She requested early retirement from the courts and planned to open her own law practice. But her application for practicing law was turned down. Frustrated but not beaten, Shirin used her eight years of unemployment to write several books and had many articles published in Iranian journals. Also during this period in the early 1980s, Shirin and Javad had two daughters, Negar and Nargess. Shirin recalls that "their childhood antics animated my life at a time when my depressing work ended and the depression of not working began."

The situation in Iran was worse than Shirin ever could have imagined when she was a student protester. Freedom of expression was denied; newspapers were shut down and the state media—including newspapers and television— were tightly controlled. Girls were denied education. And Khomeini's Intelligence Ministry arrested, tortured, or murdered many people who spoke out against the regime.

Shirin finally succeeded in obtaining a lawyer's license in 1992, and immediately set up her own practice. She began to take on politically sensitive human rights cases that many Iranian lawyers would not dream of touching. When asked why, she responded, "Who else would do it?" Shirin sees her role as a spokesperson for "silent people."

In 2000, while investigating a death squad that had murdered many Iranians, Shirin discovered something shocking. While reading through thousands of documents, she came across a familiar name on the hit list of murder targets—her own. Nonetheless she courageously continued. Shirin's efforts led to the conviction of a few members of the assassination squad; however, the government halted the investigation before her work was completed. "No senior official ever faced prosecution," wrote an angered Shirin.

In November 2003, Shirin agreed to represent the family of murdered Canadian photojournalist Zahra Kazemi, who died in police custody in Iran in July of that year. Shirin's involvement in the case guaranteed that the woman's death received high-profile coverage, even though the circumstances surrounding the murder were never resolved in a satisfying way.

After the revolution that brought Ayatollah Khomeini to power, many of Shirin's friends left Iran. She chose to stay, however, and to use her skills and influence as both a lawyer and a writer. She wanted to develop an interpretation of Islamic law that would uphold human rights rather than limit them. Shirin felt anger toward family and friends who left the country. "I refused to write letters to those who had left . . . When someone leaves Iran, it's as though that person has died to me." She says, "Certainly everyone is free to choose where they want to live. Life in Iran is very difficult . . . But let me give you an example. If your mother who is old gets sick, do you leave her on the corner of the street? And then try and find yourself a younger mother? Or would you try to help your old, sick mother to improve and feel better? Your nation, your homeland, to me is like a mother."

In 2003, Shirin Ebadi was awarded the Nobel Peace Prize. She is the first Iranian to win the prize and the first Muslim woman. Shirin shared the honor with all of the people who have worked with her on behalf of peace and human rights.

Blogging is very popular among Iranian youth—two-thirds of Iran's population is under the age of 25. Freedom of expression is limited and regulated in Iran, and blogs provide a way for young people to express their thoughts and ideas. In 2000, there were an estimated 700,000 Iranian blogs, and Persian is one of the five most popular languages for blogging.

Jody Williams, Betty Williams, Shirin Ebadi,
Máiread Corrigan Maguire, and Wangari Maathai

She said, "Muslim women around the world and all of those who have worked for the cause of human rights in Iran are partners in this award."

The Nobel committee paid tribute to Shirin's courage, noting that she had "never heeded the threat to her own safety." It's true that one of the most surprising aspects of Shirin's life is that she has not "disappeared," as so many of the government's opponents have. She continues her work, despite the fact that her outspokenness has meant her life is in danger. Shirin has survived two assassination attempts and was imprisoned in Iran for "disturbing public opinion." She believes that her international profile has helped to protect her.

Despite living with constant fear, Shirin remains optimistic about the possibility of positive change in Iran. She says, "At the beginning of the revolution, the maximum percentage of women in the universities was 25 percent. [Now], 24 years later, 63 percent of our university population is female . . . The feminist movement in Iran is very strong at this time and we will succeed in changing the laws."

Shirin teaches law at the University of Tehran, and students come from around the world to take her courses on protecting human rights. She has also taught these courses and others—on Islam and women's roles—at colleges and universities across North America and Europe.

In 2004, Shirin filed a lawsuit against the U.S. Department of the Treasury. The U.S. government had imposed sanctions, making all trade with Iran illegal. This included the publishing of books written by Iranians, which meant that Shirin wasn't permitted to publish her memoir, *Iran Awakening: A Memoir of Revolution and Hope*, in the U.S. After a long legal battle, in which Shirin argued that this ban violated the rights of American readers, she won the case. Her memoir was published in the U.S. in 2006, and has since been translated into eighteen different languages.

Speaking on her motivation for writing the book, Shirin says, "I wanted to introduce [North] American women to Iranian women and our lives. I'm not from the highest echelons of society, nor the lowest. I'm a woman who is a lawyer, who is a professor at a university, who won the Nobel Peace Prize. At the same time, I cook. And even when I'm about to go to prison, one of the first things I do is to make enough food and put it in the fridge for my family."

Wangari Maathai

Nobel Peace
Prize Laureate, 2004

Mama Miti—The "Mother of Trees"

Wangari Muta Maathai was born in 1940 in Nyeri, Kenya, in the lush foothills of Mount Kenya. Her farming family, members of the Kikuyu community, lived in a mud-walled house surrounded by fig and banana trees, fertile fields of maize and beans, and clean, flowing streams.

As a child, Wangari felt a deep love of the natural world. She fondly remembers tending to her family's sheep and goats with her siblings. They also harvested the leaves of the wild *managu*—a medicinal plant—which they would sell to people from the neighboring villages. Wangari feasted on

> "People often ask what drives me. Perhaps the more difficult question would be: what would it take to stop me?"
>
> —Wangari Maathai

the succulent berries that grew among the managu leaves, and recalls that "nothing in life was more pleasant than to be asked to take the animals into the fields."

Wangari's mother encouraged her to keep her own garden, and instructed her not to "idle around during the rains, plant something." Wangari says, "I grew up close to my mother, in the field, where I could observe nature. Whatever she did, I did—the traditional women's tasks, fetching water and gathering firewood. She was my anchor in my life."

Wangari's love of nature and her appreciation of the everyday tasks of women gave her the strength to fight back when, as an adult, she saw the environment being destroyed and women being oppressed.

Most girls in Wangari's village didn't go to school. Wangari's two older brothers attended classes, and one day the oldest asked, "How come Wangari doesn't go to school like the rest of us?" Their parents agreed to let her enroll, and at age seven, she learned to read and write. After two years at the local school, Wangari moved away from her family to attend St. Cecilia's, a Catholic boarding school. Wangari recognized that it was a rare gift to be able to attend school, and understood that it probably meant financial struggles and extra work for her family, especially for her mother.

Wangari consistently placed at the top of her class. When she visited her home, however, she never shied away from the hard, gritty work of the farm. This impressed her family's neighbors, who had expected her to turn her back on her family once she was exposed to higher learning. Instead,

Wangari became a role model for many of the young girls in her village, whose parents encouraged them to "study hard and be like her."

In 1960, Wangari received a scholarship to study at Mount St. Scholastica College in Kansas, where she obtained a degree in biology. She continued her studies at the University of Pittsburgh, earning a Masters of Science.

Wangari's time in the United States coincided with the early days of the women's movement, and she embraced that mind-opening energy and excitement. As well, particularly in Pittsburgh, she witnessed the damage caused by one hundred years of industrial pollution, including the soot-blackened houses and buildings. She also became aware of the developing environmental movement and of attempts to heal the damage caused by the pollution.

When Wangari returned to Kenya in 1965, the experiences that she'd had in the U.S. allowed her to see the environmental degradation in her homeland in a new light. This damage had been accumulating for a long time.

Until 1963, Kenya was a British colony. Before the arrival of the Europeans, the rich Kenyan highlands and fertile valleys were lush with native trees that bore figs, bananas, mangos, and papayas; dense shrubbery provided berries and nuts; thorn and cedar trees provided firewood and building materials; local people had gardens and small fields where they could grow green vegetables, sweet potatoes, and beans to feed their families. Plenty of rain and clear, clean streams allowed the plants to grow.

The British and other European colonists introduced cash crops, which were grown for export, to the fertile highlands. Enormous coffee and tea plantations soon covered the slopes of Mount Kenya, where native Kenyans used to grow many different local crops and raise their families.

The colonists also developed a timber industry. As a

child, Wangari remembers watching huge natural forests disappear into enormous bonfires, not understanding the changes that these fires would bring. Native forests were cleared and replaced with orderly plantations of eucalyptus and pine trees, which could be harvested and sold for export. To encourage the spread of these newly introduced species, the settlers provided seedlings to the locals, who enthusiastically replaced their own native species, in hopes of earning new income.

But these new and fast-growing trees wiped out the local ecosystem, destroyed the naturally efficient groundwater system, and displaced wildlife. Rains washed away unprotected topsoil, rivers became clogged with silt, and some of the rich farms that had sustained families and whole communities turned into desert. Streams dried up, and wildlife died.

Although most of the farmland was still owned by foreign settlers even after the colonial period, some individual Kenyans were able to own and farm small parcels of land, as Wangari's family did. However, because of the environmental degradation, rural families were struggling with a lack of basic resources such as firewood, building materials, and clean drinking water. Because forests were depleted, women were forced to walk further to find wood for cooking and building. Because rivers and streams were degraded, it took more time to collect water. Because fields were undernourished, livestock was starving.

When Wangari returned to Kenya from the U.S., she could see these problems but did not yet understand her role in finding the solution.

In the midst of this troubling landscape, Wangari carried on with her life. She started working in the Department of Veterinary Anatomy at the University College of Nairobi. She also became engaged to marry Mwangi Mathai, a businessman who, like Wangari, had studied in the States. Wangari

went to Germany for two years to continue her studies, and they made plans to marry when she returned.

In 1969 Wangari returned to Kenya for her wedding and to complete her Ph.D., becoming the first woman in Central or East Africa to earn that designation. She continued teaching and eventually became Chair of the Department of Veterinary Anatomy, another first for an African woman. She also supported her new husband's political career—he had decided to run for Parliament—and they started a family. In 1974, Wangari gave birth to a son, the first of their three children.

Wangari was very accomplished, but she also found that she was discriminated against because she was a woman. At the university, she and a female colleague discovered that their housing, health insurance, and pension benefits were significantly less than those of men in similar positions. They were the first two female professors in the department, and assumed that when they brought this to the attention of the administration, their salaries would be adjusted. Instead, they were forced to take the university to court. They lost the challenge, but—perhaps just to keep them quiet—the university gave Wangari and her colleague full benefits. The same privilege was not extended to other women faculty, however. In fact—fearing the wrath of their husbands—no other women would agree to join them in their battle.

> "I do not embrace the fear that so often stops us from pursuing our goals. Those of us who understand, who feel strongly, must not tire. We must not give up. We must persist. I always say that the burden is on those who know. Those who don't know are at peace. It's those of us who know that get disturbed and are forced to take action."
>
> —Wangari Maathai

Wangari Maathai

Wangari soon became involved with the National Council of Women of Kenya (NCWK) and the Environment Liaison Centre, a coalition of international organizations. Through this work, she started to understand more clearly the direct connection between the environment and women's lives. She knew that women in rural Africa are usually the primary caretakers in their families, and they are also often the first to become aware of environmental damage. As families in Kenya adjusted to the presence of cash crops and coped with the depletion of their native forests and farms, rural women had little choice but to feed their families easily obtained processed foods such as white bread, white flour, and white rice. These foods were practical and could be purchased rather than grown, but they had little nutritional value. The health of native Kenyans was suffering because they weren't eating enough fresh green vegetables and vitamin-rich fruits.

Wangari needed to get to the root of the problem. She said, "I didn't sit down and ask myself, 'Now let me see; what shall I do?' It just came to me: 'Why not plant trees?'"

In 1977, Wangari founded the Green Belt Movement (GBM), a grassroots organization with the double goal of protecting the environment and providing opportunities for women to improve their lives. Wangari's plan was to provide seeds to rural women. The idea was that these women would be taught to grow seedlings for indigenous trees. Then they would be paid for their seedlings, which would be distributed and planted. As they matured, these trees would provide wood for cooking and for building fences for livestock; they would protect watersheds and farmers' topsoil; fruit trees would provide food.

Selling the idea wasn't easy. Government workers laughed at the notion that untrained women could do the work of trained foresters. "It took me a lot of days and nights," Wangari says, "to convince people that women could improve their environment without much technology or without many financial resources."

Wangari and her supporters, which included the NCWK, put the plan into action, and the results were obvious. Not only did the women who were involved in the program soon have access to new sources of food, fuel, and shelter, but also income and employment opportunities were created, soil conditions and the watershed were improved, and women were empowered. Wangari says, "I placed my faith in the rural women of Kenya from the very beginning, and they have been key to the success of the GBM."

Suddenly, in the midst of this success, and while she was still working at the university, Wangari's husband filed for divorce. Although he had supported her career as long as she could also be a quiet and obedient "political wife," he didn't approve of her new preoccupation. She was, he declared, "too educated, too strong, too successful, too stubborn, and too hard to control."

Wangari was devastated by the divorce and, to add to the insult, when she was quoted in the media suggesting that the judge who granted the divorce was corrupt, she was arrested and thrown into a maximum-security jail. She was released after three days, knowing that she had been used as an example for other African women who might dare to speak out against their husbands or the government. (Wangari's husband also wanted her to stop using his name. Instead, she added an extra "a" to Mathai.)

Meanwhile, the GBM's efforts continued to expand. Wangari encouraged women to collect their own seeds so that they wouldn't be dependent on the free ones, and eventually groups of women were developing their own nurseries. The initiative spread across the country, so that farmers, schools, churches, and other organizations were able to apply the basic GBM principles in their own communities. Today, more than six hundred community groups and several hundred thousand people are responsible for more than six thousand tree nurseries throughout Kenya. With at least thirty million trees planted across Kenya, the GBM is one of the world's most innovative environmental programs.

In 1986, the United Nations Environment Programme recognized the success of the GBM and encouraged its leaders to share their experiences with other groups in Africa. The Pan African Green Belt Network was developed, and Wangari's vision reached even further.

As the GBM's success spread, the government of Kenya sat up and took notice. Wangari jokes that "eventually the movement became so powerful that the government saw the need to ban it." President Daniel arap Moi's single-party regime didn't like that members of the GBM were planting ideas as well as trees. They were empowering women, speaking out against dangerous environmental practices, and fighting for democracy. Many African men, in particular, thought that Wangari was stepping too far outside of a woman's proper role. The president declared that she was a "threat to the order and security of the country."

As Wangari continued to fight for women's rights,

environmental protection and democracy in Kenya, President Moi made personal attacks against her, declaring that she "had insects in her head," and suggesting that she was not a "proper woman."

Because of her political actions, Wangari was assaulted, arrested, and imprisoned. Once she was charged with treason, a crime that carries the death penalty in Kenya. This was one of her most challenging battles. She remembers, "I did not have a blanket and I was alone in the [wet, filthy] cell. I was also fifty-two years old, arthritic in both knees, and suffering from back pain. In that cold, wet cell my joints ached so much that I thought I would die." She was eventually released.

In one of the most violent incidents, Wangari was severely beaten at a tree-planting demonstration outside of Karura Forest, an area that Wangari and many others had been struggling to protect. They were attacked with whips and stones, and the police—who were standing by and watching—did nothing to protect them. When the police demanded that Wangari register her complaint on paper, she signed her documents with a fierce X, using fresh blood from her head wound.

In 2002, Kenya held its first democratic elections in many years. Wangari had been persuaded to run for the democratic National Rainbow Coalition. Her campaign slo-

November 28, 2007 was an international day of celebration. The Billion Tree Campaign reached its formidable goal of planting one billion trees worldwide. This global initiative, which is now working toward a billion more trees, was inspired by a challenge from Wangari Maathai. In response to a corporation which boasted that it was going to plant a million trees, she said, "That's great, but what we really need is to plant a billion trees."

gan was "Rise Up and Walk," a quote from the Bible that was meant to inspire Kenyans to work together to establish a responsible, accountable government. In a clear endorsement of her struggles, electors in Wangari's riding gave her more than ninety-eight percent of the vote. She became Assistant Minister for the Environment and Natural Resources, and she continued in that role until 2005, when her party was defeated.

In 2004, nearly thirty years after she founded the Green Belt Movement, Wangari was awarded the Nobel Peace Prize. She congratulated the Committee for its courageous decision to give the award to an environmentalist. She praised their effort to "broaden the understanding of peace" and in her acceptance speech, she acknowledged that "there can be no peace without equitable development; and there can be no development without sustainable management of the environment in a democratic and peaceful space."

She rejoiced with her friends and neighbors, and celebrated by planting a tree in Nyeri, near her home in Kenya. Wangari, affectionately known as "Mama Miti"—"Mother of Trees"—recalls, "After I heard the news I looked at peaceful Mount Kenya . . . and the poor mountain where our forefathers worshipped seemed to look at me and say, 'Thank you for helping me.'"

What You Can Do

How You Can Be a Troublemaker for Peace

Check out the website of the **Nobel Women's Initiative**, especially the "Links" and "Take Action" pages. You'll find up-to-date information about important issues and organizations around the world, with suggestions for how you can get involved.
www.nobelwomensinitiative.org

Go to the website of the **Women's International League for Peace and Freedom** (WILPF)—most countries have their own chapter—and find out what campaigns they are working on. Look at their "Take Action!" section for suggestions about ways that you can get involved.
www.wilpf.int.ch/world/

PeaceJam is a very cool organization started by Nobel Peace Prize winners, and dedicated to creating opportunities for

young people to create change. Make sure you read their "Global Call to Action for the Youth of the World."
www.peacejam.org

Amnesty International is always looking for more members, especially people to write letters about important human rights issues. The international site includes links to individual country sites.
www.amnesty.org

Idealist.org is a goldmine of socially responsible ideas, organizations and information. Check them out.
www.idealist.org

Read some of the books that have won the **Jane Addams Book Award**, and talk to your friends about the ideas you find there.
http://home.igc.org/~japa/jacba/index_jacba.html

Visitors to the **Clear Landmines** website can make free daily donations to the effort to eradicate landmines. And then have a look at the Youth Action Forum on the **International Campaign to Ban Landmines** website.
www.clearlandmines.com
www.icbl.org/youth

Plant a tree and contribute to the United Nations Environmental Program's **Billion Tree Campaign**. Register your pledge and record the number of trees you planted on their website.
www.unep.org/billiontreecampaign

Be aware of what's happening **in your neighborhood, your town, your country, and around the world**—and then get involved. Is there a Peace March? Put on your walking shoes. A letter-writing campaign? Get your fingers tapping. A fundraising bake sale? Cook up some cookies for the cause, or buy a pie for your neighbors—and make sure they know why.

Hold a **fundraising campaign** for your favorite cause. Most NGOs operate on a shoestring budget and every nickel counts. Use your imagination to come up with an event or a plan for gathering money, and then use your event to spread the word about the important work that is happening around the world.

Raise your voice on behalf of world peace, a healthier environment, human rights, and social justice. **Speak your mind, stay informed, and get involved**. There are literally thousands of ways to make a difference. Remember what Jody Williams said: it's hard work. Often it takes courage. And sometimes you have to be a troublemaker.

Sources and Resources

General Resources

These websites have some great information about the Nobel Peace Prize and the women (and men) who have received it:

www.nobelprize.org
This is the official site of the Nobel organization. Follow the link to the Peace Prize site and browse through stories and information, as well as presentation speeches, acceptance speeches, and Nobel lectures.

www.nobelwomensinitiative.org
This is the website of the Nobel Women's Initiative, an organization established by Nobel Peace Laureates Jody Williams, Shirin Ebadi, Wangari Maathai, Rigoberta Menchú Tum, Betty Williams and Máiread Corrigan Maguire. It is updated regularly with their current activities and news about world events that they think you should be aware of.

www.almaz.com
The Nobel Prize Internet Archive is an unofficial Nobel Prize site, with interesting biographical information and links to other informative sites.

www.britannica.com and www.answers.com are useful sources of general information about people and events.

These books are about the Nobel Peace Prize, and/or the women who have won the Nobel Peace Prize:

Abrams, Irwin. *Nobel Lectures, Peace, 1981-1990.* Singapore, World Scientific Publishing Co., 1997

Abrams, Irwin. *The Nobel Peace Prize and the Laureates: An Illustrated Biographical History, 1901-2001.* Cambridge, MA, Science History Publications, 2001

Irwin Abrams is one of the world's leading authorities on the Nobel Peace Prize and the history of the international peace movement.

Fant, Kenne (Marianne Ruuth, translator). *Alfred Nobel: A Biography.* (New York, NY, Arcade Publishing, 1991/1993)

Hicks Stiehm, Judith. *Champions for Peace: Women Winners of the Nobel Peace Prize.* Lanham, MD, Rowman and Littlefield, 2006

Price Davis, Anita et al. *Women Nobel Peace Prize Winners.* Jefferson, NC, McFarland & Co., 2006

Zelben, Jane. *Paths to Peace: People Who Changed the World.* New York, NY, Dutton, 2006

Bertha von Suttner

Anonymous. "Austria: Remembering Bertha." Women's Feature Service, www.wfsnews.org, July 2005

Hamann, Brigitte. *Bertha Von Suttner: A Life for Peace.* Syracuse, NY, Syracuse Studies on Peace and Conflict Resolution, Syracuse University Press, 1996

Kempf, Beatrix (R.W. Last, translator). *Suffragette for Peace: The Life of Bertha von Suttner.* London, Oswald Wolff, 1972

Rappaport, Helen. "The origins of women's peace campaigning," *History Today*, March 2002

www.ppu.org.uk/learn/infodocs/people/pst_bertha.html This website of the Peace Pledge Union is useful and interesting.

Jane Addams

Addams, Jane and Norah Hamilton. *Twenty Years at Hull-House: With Autobiographical Notes* (new edition. IndyPublish, 2008).

Davis, Allen F. *American Heroine: The Life and Legend of Jane Addams.* New York, NY, Ivan R. Dee, 2000

Diliberto, Gloria. *A Useful Woman: The Early Life of Jane Addams.* New York, NY, Scribner, 1999

McPherson, Stephanie Sammartino. *Peace and Bread: The Story of Jane Adams.* New York, NY, Carolrhoda Books, 1993

www.lkwdpl.org/wihohio www.americaslibrary.gov/cgi-bin/page.cgi/aa/activists Both of these sites have interesting information about

American women activists.
http://home.igc.org/~japa/index.html
The Jane Addams Peace Association (JAPA) is the educational affiliate of the Women's International League for Peace and Freedom (WILPF). Each year, they award the Jane Addams Children's Book Awards.

www.wilpf.int.ch
International site of the Women's International League for Peace and Freedom.

Emily Greene Balch

Abbot, Margery Post. "Emily Greene Balch: Pioneering Peacemaker (1867-1961)." *Friends Journal,* June 2001

Allcock, John B. and Antonia Young Black. *Lambs and Grey Falcons: Women Travellers in the Balkans.* Bradford, UK, Bradford University Press, 1991

Balch Greene, Emily. *Our Slavic Fellow Citizens.* New York, NY, Arno Press, 1969

Lambert, Tara S. "Emily Greene Balch: Crusader for Peace and Justice." M.A. Thesis, Marshall College, 2002

Randall, Mercedes M. *Improper Bostonian: Emily Greene Balch.* New York, NY, Twayne Publishers, 1964

www.nwhm.org/Education/egbalch.html

Máiread Corrigan Maguire and Betty Williams

Corrigan, Máiread, *The Vision of Peace: Faith and Hope in Northern Ireland.* Maryknoll, NY, Orbis Books, 1999

Deutsch, Richard (Jack Bernard, translator), *Máiread Corrigan. Betty Williams.* New York, NY, Barron's, 1977

Ling, Bettina and Sarah Buscher. *Máiread Corrigan and Betty Williams: Making Peace in Northern Ireland.* Women Changing the World Series, New York, NY, Feminist Press, 1999

Mitchell, George and Susan Muaddi Darraj. *Máiread Corrigan and Betty Williams: Partners for Peace in Northern Ireland.* New York, NY, Chelsea House, 2006

www.peacepeople.com
Peace People, the organization founded by Maguire and Williams.

www.centersofcompassion.org
World Centers of Compassion for Children, the organization founded by Betty Williams.

Mother Teresa
Clucas, Joan. *Mother Teresa.* New York, NY, Chelsea House, 1988

Egan, Eileen and Kathleen Egan. *Prayertimes with Mother Teresa: A New Adventure in Prayer.* New York, NY, Doubleday, 1989

Mother Teresa and Brian Kolodiejchuk. *Mother Teresa: Come Be My Light.* New York, NY, Doubleday, 2007

Muggeridge, Malcolm. *Something Beautiful for God.* London, UK, Collins, 1971

No credit. "Saints Among Us." *TIME* Magazine, Dec. 29, 1975

Spink, Kathryn. *Mother Teresa: A Complete Authorized Biography.* San Francisco, CA, Harper, 1997

Weiss, Ellen and Tina Walski. *Mother Teresa: A Life of Kindness.* London, UK, Bellwether Media, 2007

www.motherteresa.org
Mother Teresa of Calcutta Center official site.

Alva Myrdal
Bok, Sissela. *Alva Myrdal: A Daughter's Memoir.* Massachusetts, Addison-Wesley, 1991

Ekerwald, Hedvig. "Alva Myrdal. Making the Private Public." *Acta Sociologica*, vol. 43, no. 4, 2000

Herman, Sondra R. "From International Feminism to Feminist Internationalism. The Emergence of Alva Myrdal, 1936-1955." *Peace & Change*, vol. 18, no. 4, 1993

Myrdal, Alva with V. Klein. *Women's Two Roles, Rev. ed.* London, UK, Routledge & Kegan Paul, 1968

Myrdal, Alva. *Dynamics of European Nuclear Disarmament.* Nottingham, UK, Spokesman, 1981

Myrdal, Alva. *Nation and Family. Second edition.* Cambridge, MA, MIT Press, 1965

Myrdal, Alva. *The Game of Disarmament: How the United States and Russia Run the Arms Race.* New York, NY, Pantheon, 1976, revised 1982

Myrdal, Alva. *War, Weapons and Everyday Violence.* Manchester, NH, University of New Hampshire Press, 1977

Aung San Suu Kyi

Aung San Suu Kyi with Vaclav Havel, Desmond M. Tutu, and Michael Aris. *Freedom from Fear and other Writings*. New York, NY, Penguin Books, 1995

Kyi, Aung San Suu and Alan Clements. *The Voice of Hope*. New York, NY, Seven Stories Press, 1997

Kyi, Aung San Suu. *Letters from Burma*. New York, NY, Penguin Books, 1998

Kyi, Aung San Suu. *Aung San of Burma*. Gartmore, Scotland, Kiscadale Publications, 1995

Parenteau, John. *Prisoner for Peace: Aung San Suu Kyi and Burma's Struggle for Democracy*. Greensboro, NC, Morgan Reynold's Inc, 1994

Victor, Barbara. *The Lady: Aung San Suu Kyi: Nobel Laureate and Burma's Prisoner*. London, UK, Faber & Faber, 2002

Wintle, Justin. *Perfect Hostage: A Life of Aung San Suu Kyi*. London,UK, Hutchinson, 2007

www.dassk.com/index.php
Daw Aung San Suu Kyi website

www.uscampaignforburma.org/assk
U.S. campaign for Burma

Rigoberta Menchú Tum

Farah, Douglas. "Indian From Guatemala Wins Nobel Peace Prize; Rigoberta Menchú Avid Rights Defender." *The Washington Post,* October 1992

Gaines, Judith. "Nobel prize winner called charismatic in Guatemala effort." *The Boston Globe,* October 1992

McConahay, Mary Jo. "Rigoberta Menchú Tum." *The Progressive,* January 1993

Menchú Tum, Rigoberta. *I, Rigoberta Menchú: An Indian Woman in Guatemala.* New York, NY, Verso, 1987

Menchú Tum, Rigoberta. *Crossing Borders: An Autobiography.* New York, NY, Verso, 1998

NACLA editors. "An Interview with Rigoberta Menchú Tum." *NACLA Report on the Americas,* May/June 1996

Nelan, Bruce W. "Strike Against Racism." *TIME* Magazine, October 1992

Randall, Margaret. "Eyes on the prizewinner." *The Women's Review of Books,* September 1998

Zarembo, Alan, "Trouble for Rigoberta (Nobel laureate and Guatemalan activist Rigoberta Menchú)." *Newsweek International,* June 1999

www.frmt.org
Rigoberta Menchú Tum Foundation

Jody Williams
Williams, Jody. *After the Guns Fall Silent: The Enduring Legacy of Landmines.* Oxfam, 1995

This is an interesting interview with Jody Williams:
"Nobel Laureate Revisits Land Mine Debate" *Globe and Mail,* November 30, 2007

www.icbl.org
International Coalition to Ban Landmines

www.banminesusa.org
United States Campaign to Ban Landmines

Shirin Ebadi
Chu, Jeff."Ten Questions for Shirin Ebadi." *TIME Magazine,* May 8, 2006

Ebadi, Shirin and Azadeh Moaveni. *Iran Awakening: From Prison to Peace Prize: One Woman's Struggle at the Crossroads of History.* New York, NY, Vintage, 2007

Hubbard-Brown, Janet. *Shirin Ebadi: Champion for Human Rights in Iran.* New York, NY, Chelsea House, 2007

Pal, Amitabh. "Shirin Ebadi: The Progressive Interview." *The Progressive,* September 1, 2004

Wangari Maathai
Ahmad, Iftikhar. "Nobel Peace Laureate Wangari Maathai." *Social Education,* January 2005

Goodman, Amy. "Unbowed: Nobel Peace Laureate Wangari Maathai on Climate Change, Wares for Resources, the Greenbelt Movement and More." www.democracynow.org, October 2007

Gilson, Dave. "Root Causes: An Interview with Wangari Maathai." *Mother Jones,* January 2005

Maathai, Wangari. *Unbowed: A Memoir.* New York, NY, Vintage, 2007

Maathai, Wangari. *The Green Belt Movement: Sharing the Approach and the Experience.* New York, NY, Lantern Books, 2003

Mwakugu, Noel. "Locals Toast 'Mama Miti's Famous Win." BBC News, December 2004

Pal, Amitabh. "Wangari Maathai: The Progressive Interview." *The Progressive,* May 2005

Stone, Judith. "Force of Nature: Wangari Maathai." *O, The Oprah Magazine,* June 2005

Yahgulanaas, Michael Nicolls, Wangari Maathai, The Dalai Lama. *Flight of the Hummingbird: A Parable for the Environment.* Vancouver, BC, Greystone Books, 2008

www.greenbeltmovement.org
The official website of The Greenbelt Movement. Read their blog for updates on Wangari Maathai's activities.

Photo Credits

p. 12: Wikimedia Commons

p. 15: © Library of Congress

p. 24: DN-0064814, Chicago Daily News negatives collection, Chicago Historical Society

p. 27: © Corbis

p. 37: © Corbis

p. 42: © Ivan Suvanjieff/The Nobel Women's Initiative

p. 46: © Judy Rand/The Nobel Women's Initiative

p. 49: © Corbis

p. 58: © Wikimedia Commons

p. 63: © Corbis

p. 73: © Corbis

p. 82: © lewishamdreamer

p. 87: © Ivan Suvanjieff/The Nobel Women's Initiative

p. 96: © Marcia Thompson

p. 99: © Corbis

p. 102: © Japanese Campaign to Ban Landmines

p. 106: © Judy Rand/The Nobel Women's Initiative

p. 108: © Micheline Pelletier /The Nobel Women's Initiative

p. 109: © Dr Ghulam Nabi Kazi

p. 118: © Judy Rand/The Nobel Women's Initiative

p. 121: © Martin Rowe

p. 126: © Judy Rand/The Nobel Women's Initiative

Acknowledgments

Thanks to Colin Thomas. If there was a Nobel Prize for Editing, he'd have a medal. And thanks to Caitlin Mooney-Fu for her patience and support. We wrote much of this book while we were in Máncora, Peru, volunteering for Para el Mundo (www. paraelmundo.org), an NGO run by a group of extraordinary and dedicated people. Occasionally our work on the book distracted us from our responsibilities there and from the wonderful people who surrounded us. We trust that the book will help to fill out the contribution we made. And finally, we hope that these stories will inspire the girls and young women we know and love to be troublemakers for peace—especially our daughter, Caitlin; our nieces Morgan, Zola, Tara, and Segovia; and our friends Alexandra and Jackeline in Peru, and Bow, Emily, and Haedy in Canada.